DREAM ISLAND

DREAM ISLAND

A Record of the Simple Life

by

R. M. LOCKLEY

H. F. & G. WITHERBY LTD

This edition first published
in Great Britain 1988 by
H. F. & G. WITHERBY LTD,
14 Henrietta Street, London WC2E 8QJ

The illustrations by C. F. Tunnicliffe are
reproduced by permission of J. M. Dent Ltd

British Library Cataloguing in Publication Data
Lockley, R. M. (Ronald Mathias), *1903–*
Dream island: a record of a simple life.
1. Natural history. Lockley, R.M. (Ronald
Mathias), 1903–
I. Title
508′.092′4

ISBN 0-85493-162-7

Typeset in Great Britain by Centracet
and printed in Finland by Werner Soderstrom Oy

Contents

	Foreword by Lucy Irvine	*page* 7
I	Day-Dreams	11
II	Dream Island	15
III	An Unexpected Partner	25
IV	The Boat is Named	30
V	No Enemy but Winter—and Rough Weather	36
VI	Winter Work	40
VII	Lower Island Lodge	46
VIII	The Wreck of the *Alice Williams*	50
IX	Henry Samples the High Seas	55
X	*Alice* Signs her last Crew	60
XI	The Wheelhouse	66
XII	A Natural Cinema	71
XIII	House-Building	77
XIV	Wedding Day	82
XV	Promised Lands	84
XVI	The Amenities of Grassholm	90
XVII	We Visit the Bishops	95
XVIII	We Entertain	103
XIX	Wreck	108
XX	The Story of the Shearwater	114

XXI	A Rabbit's Life	121
XXII	The Adventure of the Newly Discovered Passage	126
XXIII	We Add to Our Number	131
XXIV	The *Storm-Petrel* in Jeopardy	140
XXV	A November Gale	147
XXVI	Hard Times for the Birds	153
XXVII	Happily Ever After	159
	Index	165

Foreword

by Lucy Irvine

'. . . It was . . . lonely and inaccessible . . . there was no safe harbour . . . tides swept strongly on all sides . . . In bad weather it was impossible to get near . . . All this attracted me immensely.'

This is the voice of a young man in the late 1920s, only a few years out of school, who had nothing more substantial under his belt than a little amateur farming and bird-watching before setting out to live on the lovely but at times decidedly inhospitable island of Skokholm off the Pembrokeshire coast. It is also, I believe, the secret voice of many of us, for the dream of remote island living, however difficult, arouses yearnings so wistful and profound they might almost be termed instinctive. And it is timeless and knows no age limits. It is no secret that I have been a victim of that dream and when a battered first edition of *Dream Island* landed on my desk with a request for comments, I began reading at once—although not without caution. There are, after all, quite a few island adventure stories around.

I did not stop reading until way past my bedtime, feeding the baby with the book cradled in the other arm and risking damaging the elderly dust jacket by steaming it in the bath. What made it so hard to put down? High adventure? Brilliant writing? Suspense? No. *Dream Island* is, indisputably, the story of an adventure, but a less calculated adventure story one could not find. 'Young Lockley' as the local mainlanders dubbed him, writes of the joys and perils of small boat sailing, the ups and downs of making a living by rabbit snaring and the extraordinary nesting habits of the shearwater with an infectious schoolboy zest and lack of pretension that make for sheer reading pleasure. If the language waxes a touch romantic/archaic at times one forgives him: the lad got carried away and one is delighted to be carried with him. There is no shortage of real life romance, either. '. . . As long as we had the birds, the flowers and the sea, the living, however precarious in one way, would be constant delight in all others.' The 'we' refers to his island companion, 'one Doris', daughter of a former neighbour on the mainland, whom he vows to marry—on the day, we are discreetly given to understand, that he loses his celibacy—exactly one year hence. He also promises to have a home fit for her to live in on the island by that time. And he sticks to his word.

The first half of the book describes numerous, often hazardous crossings to and from the island in the *Storm Petrel*, a tiny sailboat aided by a 2 h.p. engine christened The Infant. Information is given on the flora and fauna to be found on Skokholm and there are details of house building operations. There is also the story of a genuine 20th-century wreck. One almost sees evidence of a *Boy's Own* enthusiast in the almighty hand that guided the *Alice Williams*, a schooner carrying 200 tons of 'black diamonds' (coal) on to those particular rocks. As in *Robinson Crusoe*, every available part of the wreck was put to good use. Ms *Castaway* was, nostalgically, green with envy.

The second half tells of Doris's arrival on the island and a most unusual honeymoon spent largely at sea in the valiant *Storm Petrel*, stopping off here and there on rarely visited Atlantic islets—one with a fascinating gannet colony—and playing postman to lonely lighthouse keepers. Then life 'happily ever after' begins in earnest and Lockley takes us through the seasons, from an idyllic 'at home' cricket match in August to desperate hard times for the birds amid the snow.

This is, that rare thing, the story of a dream come true. It is a little gem of an experience captured in a little gem of a book.

Meikleburn
March 1988

CHAPTER I

Day-Dreams

To dwell alone with birds and flowers in some remote place where they were plentiful and undisturbed was an ambition early cherished in schooldays; as soon as I began to look at, and watch, and so finally to love nature.

This desire became my daily dream as I grew up. In turn I envied the Swiss Family Robinson, the Coral Islanders, and Robinson Crusoe. I wished intensely to become a Crusoe. My day-dreams led me on wondrous expeditions alone in an open boat, and landed me on isolated bird-islands, where I dwelt my hermit-life in complete happiness. I built my little hut, kept my goats and my garden, and spent my days in watching and taming birds.

As I learned more about birds and read more books, my dreams even definitely placed me in well-known bird-haunts. In turn I enjoyed many islands in the Hebrides, my favourite being the isolated North Ronay Isles. I was director of the National Sanctuary of Mull Island, or even of Skye, in inspired moments. I did not forget the Orkneys and Shetlands, and farther afield the Faroes, Iceland, Jan Mayen, even Spitzbergen, Bear Island, and at the other extreme

Tristan d'Acunha, Macquarie, the Savages, Azores and others.

I loved the more remote islands, but if, at any time, I had been offered one of those nearer home, such as Ramsey or Skomer, I should have been quite wild with delight, and I should not have said anything but a most happy acceptance to an offer of Steepholm, the little islet in the Bristol Channel in sight of my parental home.

These were pleasant if vain dreams, giving me much harmless amusement. I at least learned much about the distribution of birds, and carefully drew up on paper a list of birds which I would see on each of my island refuges.

I shall not mention here details of some of the very wild and unscrupulous plans which I made with a view to achieving the life of a recluse on an island, without carrying them out however.

As I grew up my choice of authors widened. I read Thoreau very thoroughly, and was so impressed that my thoughts and some actions were for some years quite influenced by his example. I resolved to imitate his austere mode of living when I at last came to dwell on my dream island.

With these dreams and thoughts I left school and rented a small farm on the outskirts of the town where my home had been. The farm was in a pleasant green valley, which attracted many birds, and in consequence I was for several years fairly happy in such an environment, having plenty of work to do. Moreover, my island actually materialized to some extent in the work I set myself to by digging a pond in one field and raising a tiny island in the centre around a venerable oak growing there. Morning and evening in summer before and after the day's work would see me with wheelbarrow, shovel and pick carrying on the great excavation which was to make an island and a pond sanctuary, I hoped, for pairs of sedge and reed warblers, moor-hens, coots, and wild ducks. The island I would plant, when finished, with bushes and trees, cover for innumerable welcome birds of every species.

However, it was undoubtedly a big task I had set myself, and would require years of labour. In the meantime, my good neighbour and friend, whom I shall call 'Admiral,' came with me once a year, at midsummer, to explore the coast of Wales.

We wandered together in Pembrokeshire, following the coast and visiting the islands one by one each year. Admiral looked at the islands with the eye of a painter, thinking of his brush and palette; I watched the birds, and in this way appeased a little my hunger for islands. Ramsey and Skomer were visited in turn, and the residents there in turn duly envied by me.

The wonderful bird-life on Skomer captivated us. We had, too, arrived in early June, when all the birds and the flowers were at their best. The island swarmed with sea birds and was carpeted with acres of bluebells, campion, thrift and primroses. It was from the fishermen who ferried us over from Marloes, the nearest mainland haven, that we learned about Skokholm, a lonely uninhabited island out in the Atlantic south of Skomer. They told us that the same birds and flowers were found as on Skomer, that the farm and the house on the island were in ruins, had been unoccupied for nearly twenty years and that, beyond casual fishermen, and the lighthousemen, nobody cared to visit the place. Apparently it was too lonely and inaccessible; the landing-place was very bad; there was no safe harbour; tides swept strongly on all sides, and to get there at all occupied an hour's steady sailing, or two or three hours of rowing. In bad weather it was impossible to get near the island.

All this attracted me immensely. I was at once impatient to explore Skokholm. We had, however, already spent two days extra in visiting Skomer, and a return to work was almost imperative. A south wind blew freshly up through Jack Sound, and we found that while this wind kept up no fisherman was willing to take us down the Sound and out to distant Skokholm.

Through the glasses this lonely island looked most attractive. The ruins of the farm buildings showed clearly in the sunshine, as well as the stone hedges of the old fields. There were wide stretches of pink where thrift flowered, and misty areas of blue where no doubt bluebells spread over the meadows. At the farthest and highest point was the white tower of the lighthouse, facing the open Atlantic which stretches, without land between, to America. The cliffs were a bright red in the sunshine, and a garland of surf beat and danced beneath them. We left Marloes vowing to return next year and make a prolonged visit to the lonely isle.

CHAPTER II

Dream Island

My dreams now centred largely on the summer holiday Admiral and I were to enjoy on the far-away and deserted isle. The time seemed slow in coming, but at last June again arrived and we set off.

There was a fresh wind blowing when we arrived at Marloes. The fisherman who agreed to take us to Skokholm shook his head over our prospects.

''Twill be rough to-morrow I'm thinkin', the way the wind is now. We can take you to Skomer if you like.'

It proved as he said, a south-westerly wind roughening the open sea where lay the inaccessible island. We spent the day partly in talking to the farmer who rented Skokholm, learning much of its history from him. Although he still rented the island from the lord of the manor, he had long ago given up visiting it. Some twenty years ago he had spent the 'happiest days of his life' living on the island with his wife, when he had undertaken a certain amount of farming with cattle and sheep. Actually the farm buildings had been in ruins when he had taken the tenancy over, and the farm had not been in proper repair since some time late in the last century. He gave us permission to enjoy ourselves as long as we pleased on Skokholm.

On the third day there was sunshine and no wind. John the fisherman and his mate walked down from Marloes with us to the haven, where the few fishermen of the village keep their boats for shell-fishing. Martinshaven that day was bright with bluebells and foxgloves, and the long walk of two miles from the village along the lane to the beach was made pleasant by the corn-bunting singing 'a-little-bit-of-bread' to us from the furze-grown hedges, and by lizards basking or darting about in the sunshine.

John's boat, the *Foxtrot*, was launched over the pebbles of the little beach, and in a few minutes we were being rowed out towards the famous Jack Sound, dreaded by mariners. We carried a supply of food, our cameras and field-glasses.

This was our first acquaintance with Jack Sound, its rocks, shoals and striving tide-races. It was not without a considerable thrill that we felt the current sweep the *Foxtrot* along with great force and carry us willy-nilly down into the open sea. Although there was no wind the water was rough at the outfall of the tide, and the boat danced and bumped unmercifully until we got clear of the strongest current.

'Now you know how 'tis she's named the *Foxtrot!*' John's mate, a voluble fellow, informed us when we were one-stepping in mid-current.

An hour-long pull followed, and another bump through the tide-race near the island had to be faced ere we reached the calm water under the island's cliffs.

All the time we had seen birds flying above or resting on the sea in the Broad Sound between Skomer and Skokholm, and now, as we drew in to the latter island, the calm water was strewn with companies of puffins, razorbills, guillemots, gulls, cormorants and other sea-fowl—a wonderful sight for a bird-lover. The puffins amused us greatly by their comical expressions. They allowed the boat to come quite close to them before giving us a last comical look of injured amazement (as it seemed to me) and diving suddenly and steeply down into the clear water. We could see them plainly, swimming under the water with short decisive movements of their half-spread wings. The groups of razorbills, black and white in smart uniforms, gave us a general howl or growl, expressive of alarm and probably annoyance before flying or diving out of our way. The gulls wheeled far above, protesting with great clamour.

The landing-place is in a southern-facing opening in the low cliffs. Here convenient steps run down to meet all states of tide. The fishermen left us at the steps, promising to fetch us in two days' time, and they rowed out of the haven to attend to their lobster-pots set along the rocky shore.

As we walked up the steep path to the fields above, shouldering our haversacks, the multitude and variety of the wild-flowers made us burst forth into spontaneous praise. The sloping banks, the cliff, the very rock, was clothed in a woven fabric of white sea campion, pink thrift, bluebells, white scurvy-grass, late primroses, blue vernal squill, cowslips, foxgloves, yellow lady's-fingers, samphire and red sea tree mallows. The whole haven, this south haven of Skokholm, glowed with the flowers, which were widely opened to the midday sun.

A path wound through bracken uphill, presently opening out upon a green meadow where bluebells flourished in stout colonies at intervals over the open grassland. The old house and buildings stood snugly sheltered from the southerly wind under a rocky eminence at the highest point of this meadow.

Although birds were running, calling and flying everywhere about us, and I was distracted by their numbers and eager to watch them, the first thing we curious human beings did was to explore the ruined buildings. There was a great fascination in exploring this ancient, storm-beaten dwelling. What manner of building had the first islanders thought fit to erect?

We dropped our packs in the sunshine outside and, not without some excitement on my part, began our exploration. With difficulty we pushed open the rotten and hingeless door of this cottage dwelling. We found ourselves in a roofless porch. Next came an ante-room with three doors leading to three rooms. The doors were rotting to dust, and we had to lift them bodily out of our way. On the right of the ante-room was a small room barely seven feet square, containing an open fireplace and a small ingle built into the wall—evidently the kitchen. There was no roof to this room, but it was occupied by a pair of blackbirds, which had four eggs in their nest on a shelf above the ingle-seat. On the left of the ante-room was another room of exactly the same small size, roofless, and floored with large slabs of red island stone. We guessed this had once been the pantry or store, for it had a tiny north-facing window. The middle door of the ante-room opened into the main room of the old dwelling, and here we were greeted by a fine state of affairs.

This living-room was floored with decaying boards, and raftered with ancient oak beams, with a sleeping loft above. The blue sky showed through many rude holes in the floor of the loft. One large window had a few good panes left, the rest boarded over and stuffed with rags.

The best part of this room was occupied by an enormous four-poster bed, built crudely out of driftwood, and on the crossboards, which served as a mattress-support, were a couple of sacks stuffed with hay and much-flattened by pressure. A ruinous old greatcoat served as a quilt. There were, besides, a rough driftwood table, two benches and a genuine old bed cupboard. On the hearth beside the ruined oven and grate were a battered kettle with partly amputated spout and handle, an old brown earthenware teapot in like case and a lately used farm-size frying-pan with fat freshly congealed in it. A few broken pieces of crockery, plates and cups to the number of half a score occupied the table in company with some malformed forks and spoons, breadcrumbs and crusts, and a noble array of shells of razorbill and three kinds of gulls' eggs. From the oaken beams hung a multitude of items: dried rabbit-skins, small sacks full or half empty, wire snares, dried birds, rags and innumerable sooty cobwebs. A shelf running along one wall was piled with rags, old gins and snares, empty pots and tins, a ruined muzzle-loader, rotten canvas and rope, twine, and finally an old family Bible—a 1763 edition. The walls were hung with crumbling plaster and cobwebs.

It was into this room that we suddenly entered and for a moment held our breaths. What manner of man lived here? I half expected to see some old miser start up from a dark corner; or perhaps some recluse, some decadent or demoralized follower of Thoreau lived here! These were my first thoughts, but nothing unusual occurred. A mouse ran boldly out upon the table to nibble the crumbs, and the swallows twittered at their nest in the airy loft above. Two doors led from this main room, one to a small roofless room occupied by a pair of wheatears and hanging tufts of flowering pearlwort on the south side, and one to a similar room, roofed partly, and containing an iron bedstead with a broken wire mattress, the whole lashed in place with canvas and rope, on the north side of the dwelling.

Out of doors there were two farm-folds surrounded by broken-down walls, and some nine outbuildings; all roofless ruins in possession of the wheatears, stone-chats, pipits and hedge-sparrows, save the partly tiled barn, the roof of which was still mostly in place.

In complete happiness Admiral and I wandered about the island. Here at last was my dream island! The flowers, stretching for acres over meadow and cliff-slope made Admiral brood over them from afar, turning the living scene to dream-pictures to store up in his memory. Half the island is divided into fields around the farmhouse, the western half, at the extreme of which stands the lighthouse, being quite as wild as nature made it, but heather, bracken and flowers stray equally over both sections of the island. The hedges are of earth supported by an outer wall of stones, the latter overgrown by moss and lichen. Rabbits have penetrated these dry walls and made burrows in all the meadows. Following the rabbits the birds, too, have made homes in the walls and the meadow-warrens.

Mr Puffin, as the fishermen call him, is the star turn of the island-birds by day in June. With his smart black wings and tail, his white starched shirt-front, his vermilion legs, his enormous red, blue and yellow-striped beak, and his profound air of importance as he looks at you with his clownish brown eye, he compels your attention. From the flat surface of the island many high outcrops of rock rose, and it was on these rocky knolls that Mr Puffin would collect each day after noon. One by one the birds, like so many white-fronted aldermen, would alight and stand close together until the rocks were thickly dotted with puffins. When I approached them they would frequently commence a restless jig with their webbed feet, 'foxtrotting', Admiral suggested, and now and then one could imagine that an extra good story was being passed around when one bird after another uttered a profound aldermanic 'Ah—ha—ha.' In his jigs Mr Puffin would sometimes turn completely around, bowing at intervals, as if to his audience, and it might then be seen that his pate was greyish, a touch which completed the aldermanic likeness.

The puffin nests in the rabbit-holes. Admiral and I found an egg being zealously incubated at the end of a burrow seven feet long. There were several exits and entrances and inter-subways to other burrows; for it was all part of a warren inhabited by other puffins, by Manx shearwaters, and, of course, by the builders and architects in the first place—I mean the rabbits.

The shearwaters, of whom I will speak later, were not seen at all during the day, but from 11 p.m. until 3 a.m., in the midnight hours, were very much in evidence. On the first night we were startled and amused by the extraordinary cooing of the shearwaters, which were sitting (on their eggs I presume) in the depths of the rabbit-burrows, and an hour or two later, just before midnight, the birds returning from the sea to their sitting mates came flying home screaming, in ever-increasing numbers, until at last, the whole island resounded with their unearthly cries. I have tried to put the cry to words:

kŭck-kŭck-kŭck-ōōōō

The birds each have a variation in tone or pitch of note, but all the cries are very harsh. Admiral said they were screaming a ferocious 'Apple-tart!' and certainly the cry of birds at some distance was not unlike this word. But the imagination had every opportunity for free rein, so wide is the variation of their weird notes. The concert was over long before sunrise.

The shearwater, the puffin and the storm-petrel are perhaps the most outstanding birds on the island, and were the species that most interested me. Of other birds there was a vast host, particularly of gulls and of oyster-catchers, and I will speak of them all in turn. Suffice it to say here that I had never been so happy in my life as I was during those three days on this wonderful bird-island, and I knew I should never be content until I lived permanently here. Admiral was less sure that he would want to live in quite so isolated a place, and he gave me wise counsel from the experience of his years, which were more than twice the number of mine. However, I was so excited that I think he knew I should not be happy until I got my wish. At any rate, in the end, he brought his sympathy and advice to bear on the problem of obtaining the island for ourselves.

We soon found that John and his fishing partner were the mysterious tenants of the old house, and that they slept there on very fine summer nights, mooring their boat off in the calm water of South Haven, and thus saving the time and labour of rowing down to the Island from Martinshaven each day. Of course it was a proceeding not without risk, and as soon as the wind increased, or backed to southward, they had to be ready to fly to the mainland.

The men came in at sunset each evening and made a supper of fried bacon and fried gulls' or razorbills' eggs. They then yarned with us for an hour before throwing themselves on the four-poster and sleeping heavily until four or five in the morning. John would snore in tune with the shearwaters that screamed over the housetop, while his mate gradually appropriated the major portion of the bed. We watched this phenomenon with interest in our waking moments, for Admiral and I slept on some hay on the floor by the fire when we were not out-of-doors with the shearwaters at night. At last, when John was in danger of falling out of bed, he would encounter the hard rail of the side, which would forcibly wake him. Thus roused he would get up, draw his boots on, stir the driftwood fire into life, and cook breakfast. A dozen eggs would be put on to boil in an old saucepan, and those found to be not too far incubated were eaten with bread and butter, and washed down with unlimited tea. The men then went out to fish, and we did not see them again until evening. The egg supply was short one evening when they came in early, so they went off to rob the gulls' nests on the island bog and the razorbills' nests on the rocky slopes of Mad Bay.

Gulls' eggs, we found, were very palatable to bird lovers' hungry stomachs. I had no qualms either when I saw how cruelly the black-backed gulls would attack and kill a puffin or a young rabbit, or rob a razorbill of its egg. There were hundreds of thieving gulls, and we had no trouble in finding their nests in the meadows and in the bog-grass. John told us they go on laying indefinitely if the eggs are taken regularly. He also brought us pollack, crab and lobster, so that we were never short of fish for our supper.

It was a sad day, therefore, when we had to tear ourselves away at last from this island of my dreams.

CHAPTER III

An Unexpected Partner

There were anxious moments when I got home to my farm. I proposed to sell my stock and plant at once, in order to realize some capital for setting up as an islander. Not without considerable difficulty, and more than one perilous interruption of the negotiations, did I at last secure the legal right to dwell in the peaceful possession and the 'quiet enjoyment' of Skokholm. Those were the two most anxious months of my life, I believe, when all was in a turmoil of negotiation, of hopes running very high at one moment and correspondingly low at another. Admiral, although he did not propose to come and live with me, being tied by family considerations, was my most faithful and true help throughout all my difficulties.

More complication was to arise, however, when one Doris learned of these plans. Hitherto Doris had been a friend with whom I exchanged ornithological notes whenever we met, as we often did, being farming neighbours a few fields apart from each other. She was wont to consult me in regard to birds, and I her in respect to wild-flowers, on which she was undoubtedly an authority.

Now, when I told her all about Dream Island and

how I proposed to live alone there, happy with my birds and the flowers, she was sad and full of envy. Even now I sometimes wonder if it was because I had an island to offer that she—well, it will suffice to say that very suddenly my lofty plan to be another Crusoe (with a Thoreauvian austereness of life) was completely annihilated. Henceforth I renounced celibacy. I took an oath on that same sunny day, a certain July 12th, that in one year's time to the very day I would have the island house fit for her to live in. We were to be married, it was agreed, on July 12th a year hence—and we would live happily ever after!

Doris had taken much for granted, had accepted my glowing accounts without reservation. Still, it was only fair that she should see the island, and admire her future home with her own eyes, for at this stage she was already planning house improvements.

Quite a cavalcade of curious relatives accompanied Doris, Admiral and myself down to Marloes. John the fisherman again launched the worthy *Foxtrot*, and ferried six of the bravest over to the island. It was a calm day, and we took two hours to cross with oars only. As we drew near the red cliffs of Dream Island we put out mackerel lines to catch our suppers, and were rewarded with both mackerel and pollack.

It was now early August, and the cliff-nesting birds, the guillemots and razorbills, had left, but there were still many puffins, gulls and oyster-catchers, and many small land-loving birds. The puffins were busy feeding their nearly fledged young, and all that afternoon could be seen bringing sprats to the nesting holes. With the aid of our glasses we could see that Mr Puffin held three or four sprats in his beak, heads all to one side, and tails to the other. Now how does he manage to arrange them so neatly? And how does he catch more than one at a time? We saw a lazy herring-gull watching the incoming puffins, and ever and anon swooping down on a bird just about to enter its hole. The puffin would then hastily drop his sprats, which the robber calmly swallowed.

Over the old island dwelling five buzzards were soaring, furnishing a sight to thrill us all. Up and up they soared, wheeling round and round without a flap of their broad wings until they were almost lost in the blue sky. We found later that the buzzards had come for a nefarious purpose, to wit to slaughter the young birds and young rabbits, and to kill any defenceless shearwater which had lost its way or been unable to rise from the bracken overnight.

All my visitors were impressed by the lovely colours of the island: the red rocks, lichened in pale green here and there, the purple heather now in flower. Only campion, of the spring flowers, remained in bloom, but there were stretches of golden-rod, ragwort, variegated wild pansies and birdsfoot trefoil.

The gloom and filth of the interior of the old house did not dismay Doris, as it did her three companions. She boldly cooked the fish in the ancient frying-pan and put good heart into all by feeding us well.

There and then she gave me directions for reconstructing the old dwelling to her liking. They were simple enough. I was to remove the partition between living-room and ante-room, thus making one large main room; to remove the wall between the little kitchen and the little room on the south side, thus making for her a reasonably large kitchen, where she might carry on in comfort the making and baking which would be inseparable from such an independent home. This, and a roof for her head, was all she asked of me, and she demanded that I should leave as much pioneer work as possible undone that she might eventually share therein.

That evening the living-room was looking trimmer than it had been for many years. The cobwebs were swept away, and a roaring driftwood fire built up.

Early in the morning we all came in from a long overnight inspection of the shearwaters and the storm-petrels, and ate our supper-cum-breakfast of fish, toast and tea with hearty appetite.

The storm-petrels we found flying like swallows everywhere on the island at night, but especially about the South Haven. Several pairs were nesting in a heap of limestones above the old lime-kiln, and we could hear the newly hatched chicks uttering a very plaintive 'peep-peep'. We uncovered one nest and found both parents tending their solitary, young downy chick. The petrels were nesting, too, in cracks and chinks in the hedge-walls, and there was even a nestling in a crack in the outside wall of the dwelling-house. It was strange to see these airy little birds, by day restless wanderers on the sea, at night flying with a quick, swallow-like grace, perfectly at home, about and over the rocks and walls where they had their young.

A strong wind came with sunrise, and the fishermen who had moored the boat in South Haven overnight came up to us at once to say that it was time to go.

Before we could make ready, however, quite a stiff wind was blowing directly into the little haven, and the waves began to rise and roar in and about it.

The fishermen leaped agilely into their boat, which was straining and tossing wildly at its moorings, and we were invited to leap after them—from the landing steps. It was an exciting moment, but at last everyone had leaped or tumbled aboard without serious mishap. Luckily the three lightkeepers, with whom we had made good friends, had come down from the lighthouse to see us off, and they held the mooring-ropes so as to assist us and to pull the boat away from the steps. They waved us good-bye, and watched us sail away swiftly before the rising summer gale.

CHAPTER IV

The Boat is Named

It was not without fully realizing the responsibility of my step, and the possible consequences, that I gave up my farm, selling what I owned, the stock and plant, to the new tenant. I knew that when I had spent my small capital I should be dependent on what I could earn by fishing round, and farming on, the island. The thought was nevertheless quite a pleasure to me. As long as we had the birds, the flowers and the sea, the living, however precarious in one way, would be a constant delight in all others.

Possession of the Island of Skokholm, described as 'comprising 250 acres or thereabouts of rough grazing', was to be obtained at Michaelmas, and on that date I gave up my farm, taking with me only the few tools and items of furniture, and the books I valued most.

The farmers of Marloes are the most hospitable folk one could wish to meet, and while I was on the mainland I never lacked a welcome or a home at any time. This was especially valuable when cold, wet and hungry after a long and stormy crossing from my island, I was assured of a warm fire, good food and a comfortable rest.

It was only a matter of a few months, I was warned, before I would be returning home, glad to be quit of a storm-bound coast, devastated day after day by gales before which nothing taller than a furze-bush survived out of doors.

As for living on the Lower Island, as the local people termed Skokholm in contradistinction to Skomer the Upper Island, if the hardy Marloes-born folk could not face it, then surely 'young Lockley', arrived out of the hinterland of town life as they supposed, would soon give it up as a bad job.

My first task before finally settling in was to find me a boat. An islander without a boat was unthinkable. To possess a boat that could carry you on expeditions both in storm and calm was to have a valuable possession I soon learned, and in the boat which I subsequently obtained, this, I think, was fairly exemplified.

John the fisherman, whom I now permanently engaged as boatman and general assistant, lent his experience to the selection of a suitable boat. I wanted a boat neither too large to be handled by two men in and about the narrow and dangerous landing-place on the island, nor too small to face the vagaries of rough tides and winds on the open sea.

So, together, we examined boats in nearly every haven and port of Pembrokeshire, condemning many. They were all either too large and heavy, or else uselessly small and without engines. In each case, too, the owner seemed to have an extravagant idea of their cash value. An engine was also essential, to help defeat contrary tides and winds.

Eventually John approved a rather small boat, about seventeen feet long, with a small 2 h.p. auxiliary engine. We were taken for a cruise in it, and as it seemed correspondingly cheap in relation to its size I bought it.

Meanwhile, these days of boat-hunting without result had made me restive to be again on my island, and one day I proposed to John that together we should take the fair north-east breeze then blowing and sail down first to see how everything was upon that delectable spot. We therefore launched the *Foxtrot*, and went down through the Sounds before the wind, under the red lugsail, and at a spirited pace.

The birds had now had the island to themselves for so many months that they were very tame when we landed. All the summer birds had left, but I was very pleased to see others in their place, including hundreds of thrushes and blackbirds, many starlings, robins and wrens, a few buzzards, falcons, and the pair of ravens, whilst about, or on, the pond great flocks of lapwing, curlew, mallard and teal. Few flowers were left, but colours still glowed in the October sunlight—red rock, green grass and thrift, russet bracken and heather.

We moored the boat in South Haven and then tried to think out the best means of keeping a boat on the island in bad weather. John told me that the former tenant used to haul his boat up from the tiny beach of red pebbles with a hand-winch, winding the boat up on a cable until it rested on the rocky cliff above high-water mark. The three lightkeepers came to give their advice, too, and were pleased to learn that someone was coming to live on the island—no doubt thinking of the increased opportunities of posting and receiving mail this would mean for them, among other considerations.

New wire would be wanted for the winch, which was still in working order, having been used fairly frequently by rabbit-catchers and fishermen. So I made a list of the many things required for our immediate use.

When we put out of South Haven on our return to the mainland the sun was setting, and a little owl called us a good-night from the red cliffs. John bade me take an oar and prepare for a stiff pull along the island shore until we reached the point—at which it would be possible to hoist sail. It was my first acquaintance with a seventeen-foot sea-sweep, and I had a very grim battle with it. Soon my wrists and back were aching badly, for the *Foxtrot* was light and resisted the wind with her high freeboard, so that, when at last we could hoist sail, and by a series of tacks with the tide make our way to the mainland, I was mightily relieved.

My newly acquired boat was one fine day, at last, delivered at Martinshaven by its late owner, and on the next day, after we had learned how to run the simple little engine, we prepared to make a journey to the island, carrying my furniture and tools, and a rabbit-catcher to work there.

There was quite a mild amount of excitement in Martinshaven when I loaded my goods and chattels. First the ponderous *Foxtrot* was filled with chairs and boxes, and then the new boat, *my* boat, was loaded.

Richard, the veteran rabbit-catcher, stepped aboard the *Foxtrot* and we pushed her afloat. Then John and I pushed off the new boat, took the *Foxtrot* in tow with a length of stout rope, and away the infant engine barked, tugging her double load slowly over the flat calm sea. Though such progress was slow we had a good tide and got down to the island in but little more than an hour.

We then proceeded to unload and carry the goods up to the old house. Next we tried hauling up my boat over the rocks, fitting the new wire cable to the winch. There were some nasty gaps in the rocks, but we bridged these with greased sticks, over which the iron-shod keel of the boat slid without difficulty. This, apparently, had been the method here from time immemorial.

When she was at last above the high-water mark of all (and stormy) tides, I admired her in her steep berth. It seemed to me something of an achievement to have hauled a boat up into that cranny in the rocks, and I named her there and then the *Storm-Petrel*; for did not she, like that other sea-farer, fly up to her home in the rocks by night?

Richard was from now on left in charge of the island, for we had to take back the empty *Foxtrot* to the mainland. Not for the first time had Richard been left thus on the Lower Island, with his supply of food; he was, indeed, one of few men accustomed in past winters to spend weeks alone here; a true philosopher and a clever man at his work.

A fresh northerly breeze had sprung up, and as we slowly pushed along with the tide it increased; but when we reached Jack Sound the north wind had already commenced to strive roughly with the north-running tide, and there was a white mass of smother on the notorious Haze or Wooltack Point. Through this we safely made our way, though soaked and jostled. When we reached Martinshaven the waves were breaking heavily on that north-facing beach, and the problem set us was how to beach two boats safely at the same moment, for no good Samaritan was there to help us pull the boats clear of the breakers.

We sprang ashore and pulled mightily at the bow-ropes of both boats, but it was an impossible task for only two. I clung to the *Storm-Petrel*'s rope, John to the *Foxtrot*'s. At one moment the boats would lie clear and dry on the pebbles as the breakers sucked backwards, then the waves came curling and breaking in with a rush, slapping the boats and trying to turn them broadside on. We hauled in a little each time the waves rushed in, but soon the boats were so full of water, and consequently so heavy that we could pull no more. My own boat was soon more than half full, and the engine quite under water: a tragedy it seemed to me. But we could do nothing now but wait for the tide to ebb, then empty the water out, and haul the boats up above high-water mark.

CHAPTER V

No Enemy but Winter—and Rough Weather

On the following day a southerly gale blew, and this was succeeded day after day by a series of gales, culminating on the seventh day with a hurricane that did much damage to roofs everywhere on the mainland. I wondered how Richard had fared on the lonely island, and whether anything would now be left of the dwelling. At least the roof, I thought, would be entirely gone.

John and I dismantled the *Storm-Petrel*'s engine, dried and cleaned it, and at last got it to function again, though it was a long time before it seemed to recover fully from its total immersion.

Nine days after we had left Richard on the island the wind abated enough for us to venture through Jack Sound, and so at long last down to my almost inaccessible home.

Under its snug outcrop of rock the dwelling had weathered the gales well, the roof having been only a little disarranged. But Richard reported that a window had blown in one night and made things so uncomfortable, also that the house had shaken so much that he had spent the rest of the night in the open. He asked me if I intended to return at once to the mainland with the dozen score of so of rabbits, some of them already stale, which he had caught for me.

I intended, however, to snatch one night in my new home. Richard looked at the weather and shook his head; however, we hauled the boat up over the crazy slipway, and before dusk I had patched up the roof with enough old tiles and rusty sheet-iron I found derelict near by to make it tolerably rainproof.

A southerly gale came that evening, moaning and whining in the patched-up window crannies. The next morning the sea leaped and thundered in fury about the island. The boat was then safely hauled up to the very wheel of the winch, for the harbour itself was one cauldron of foam and spray. This was the first day of November, and day followed day without a cessation of the gales. John went out to help Richard. It was too rough to attempt house-repairs, and so I turned my attention to the ancient garden, a walled-in area in front of the dwelling. Here, where now bracken, briar and nettle flourished, was one day to be sweetly cultivated garden. The soil was an old, cultivated loam I found, as I dug and removed the tangle of bracken and nettle-roots.

I had good company, too, while the gales whitened the sea, for the smaller birds came into the garden for shelter. A few early redwings mixed with the company, varied each day, of thrushes, blackbirds, chaffinches and meadow-pipits. Sometimes a goldfinch would alight on the garden wall, a thick bank of stone and earth; sometimes it was a greenfinch or a flock of linnets or starlings, and often a pair of choughs, rare, handsome birds that were not at all shy while on the island. At all times there were wrens busily examining the stones of the walls, and the inevitable yet welcome hedge-sparrows creeping tamely near my busy spade. Of the several robins on the island, each one in possession of its own territory, from which it drove all others of its kind, there was one so tame that it learned to come into the house for shelter and food day and night.

In the evenings the three of us sat before a roaring fire of driftwood, collected from the creeks and bays of the island. Richard and John would look at the illustrations in my bird and other books. Richard could not read or write, and it was a source of amusement for him to try and guess the names of the more familiar birds. At other times he would sit upright and silent in the armchair I had provided for his old bones, talking a little to himself and keeping the fire zealously ablaze and cheerful by gentle pokings and fuel.

I had constituted myself head cook and bottle-washer, and generally had plenty to do, but in the dancing blue and red flames of the driftwood fire I could build up my castles and dreams of the future. Out-of-doors the wind shrieked, and the sea was all a smother of white horses and wind-driven foam. From the house the view of the mainland, of Jack Sound and of Skomer, is bold and grand, but it was especially fine with the sea leaping up every cliff. Steam and sailing ships constantly passed between Skokholm and the mainland, making for the shelter of Milford Haven, at the entrance to which stands the lighthouse of St Ann's. At night this bright lantern would send its intermittent light through the window upon the wall of the little room where I slept alone.

To be on the island was a great joy to me, and the difficulties and trials that confronted me at every turn made me all the more eager to attempt to overcome them.

Many of the earlier-caught rabbits were now stale, and had to be thrown away, but at last, on the fifth of November, the wind veered to the north-west and we made haste to leave. With difficulty the boat was lowered over the crazy planks, the rabbits loaded and the engine started. No sooner had we reached the extreme point of the island, the tall Stack rock, and had begun to put across to the mainland when a gale began to spring up and we were driven back again. Our troubles were not over, however, for, in hauling the boat up again, a timber bridging over a large hole in the rocks suddenly cracked in two, letting the boat down abruptly upon a sharp rock-edge and thus tearing a nasty hole in the side.

The ever-useful John, however, mended the rent with lead, tacks and tar, and we waited for the next favourable day; but this did not come until two days later, when the weather moderated enough for us to venture again upon the sea-passage.

CHAPTER VI

Winter Work

When we had sewn an outfit of sails for the *Storm-Petrel* I was more pleased than ever to own and use her, for with her new lug and jib sails she was capable of tackling all but the roughest seas. Now when the engine was wetted by heavy spray and unwilling to function we were not dependent on oars; the sails would carry us where we wished. With both engine and sails she would drive forward at an exhilarating pace. Often there was no need to use the engine, when the gales blew us, under reefed lugsail only, across to the mainland; for it was easier to fly from the island before a southerly wind than to get back again. We seemed to get very few of those desirable northerly and easterly breezes, which, blowing from the land, could not raise an angry sea, and which were so favourable to a swift passage to my island home.

Each crossing was an adventure, and, to me, an achievement; sometimes a calm passage, but more often a rough and a swift one. We fought contrary tides by helping the engine with oars, or contrary winds by beating and tacking, the engine enabling us to sail very close to the wind. Nevertheless, we were often beaten and driven back, forced to land on unsuitable beaches or to fly back whence we came, taken aback by a stormy shift or increase of wind. There were endless setbacks and disappointments, such as rabbits lost by staleness through inability to market them, and the impossibility of returning to the island for days at a stretch.

Yet every day there was a wonderful song within me. I enjoyed every adventure, admired every mood of sea and sky, and as the days passed began to look forward to spring with the return of the summer birds, and so to summer and the many things that must come to pass then. I believe I was the happiest mortal in the world.

There were, of course, an hundred and one things to be done, and I chafed at the delay caused by being weatherbound ashore on the mainland. But I soon learned to use every fine day to cross with the rabbits, which were an important source of revenue. So that, when I had learned each intricacy of the tide and current from St Ann's Head to Jack Sound, I was more capable of judging whether we could make a favourable passage, and at what time we could return. Always I considered how to overcome the contrary tide in order to get home again on the same day, for I hated being idle on the mainland when there was so much important and interesting work to be done on the island.

The crazy slipway in South Haven was a great source of danger to the boat, and this was one of the first jobs that cried for attention. The present and past method of bridging the gaps in the rocks with greased planks, for the keel to slide over, was also a laborious business, and often the rough seas would wash them away either before the boat landed or after it had passed over them. To build a solid slip of concrete was far too expensive a project, and in winter there was a likelihood of the whole being swept out by one of the terrible groundseas that pounded into the haven after each gale. It seemed to me that the best thing to do would be to bridge the gaps with something heavy and permanent, such as a series of iron rungs bolted to the rock, so as to make a sort of ladder up which the boat could slide. John and I talked it over and finally agreed that this was the only thing to be done under the circumstances.

At last, when I had almost decided to send to the nearest foundry, many miles away, for the required angle-iron we noticed two strange-looking objects beneath the boulders in South Haven, and but a few yards from the landing-beach. A heavy groundsea had recently displaced some of the great red boulders on the beach and had brought to light two long spars, partly green with weed, partly bare through the chafing of the pebbles. They were of iron, and when we had dragged them from beneath the rocks it was plain that we had discovered the very thing we required. The two spars were of angle-iron, and must have been part of some ship's boat or barge, for John now recollected an old tale of a boat driven ashore in a gale in South Haven. These irons were evidently the sole remnant of that boat, the wood having long ago drifted away. The irons were each at least thirty feet long, and put together framed the gunwale line of the boat.

Here was a marvellous piece of good fortune for us. With considerable difficulty we hauled the heavy irons up above high-water mark, and then spent several days in cutting them up into iron rungs of the required sizes to bridge the gaps, straightening the rungs in a fire, and finally bolting them down upon the rocky slipway. We drove holes in the rock with a rock chisel and cemented the bolts into these holes, and thus, in time, achieved a ladder for the boat at almost no expense. The keel could now slide easily over greased, hardwood bars which were then permanently fixed in the angles of the iron rungs.

The sea had given us these irons, as it had given, and daily continued to give to us, enough driftwood to keep us warm with bright fires. Especially when south-easterly winds blew did the sea leave for us in South Haven, Boar's Bay, Peter's Bay, and Crab Bay, those southward-facing openings in the cliffs, a quantity of timber. It is true that nearly all of it was small and fit only for firewood, but occasionally a useful spar or plank drifted in. These I put aside to be used for the house-building. Other prizes the sea gave us also: boxes and bottles filled and empty, bunches of candles, fruit, glass floats, corks and innumerable surprises and sometimes useful items.

November and December passed, and they were months of storm and wet. But when the slipway was finished I was happier about the *Storm-Petrel*. We found we could now launch the boat over the iron ladder in quite rough water with safety, and in this way we were able to get away more often and so save the rabbit-crop. I began to love being out in the boat, sailing upon the tide-strewn sea. The cormorants, shags and gulls were pleasant company in all weathers, and sometimes we saw red-throated and great northern divers, and little auks—all wanderers from colder seas. Often, too, we went out in weather not fit for an open boat, but now that I know the sea better, and respect it more, I sometimes think with amazement of the number of times we did so venture: when the sea beat inboard, and of how many times the lee-rail was awash as we lay down to a stormy beam wind, under reefed sail.

When on the island I at once turned my attention to repairing the old barn. This building I intended to make habitable enough to live in while we were dismantling and repairing the old house. I did not intend touching the house until the spring, when I hoped for better weather, but meanwhile I tackled the barn, taking up a trowel for the first time in my life. To engage a mason, besides being an expensive business, was almost an impossibility. No one would face the work and life here in the winter, for some reason I could not entirely fathom, though I guessed at it.

John was at hand to advise, in between his usual work of assisting Richard, and by Christmas-time I had repaired the roof and walls of the barn. For mortar we dug a fine earthy sandpit under an outcrop of rock in the middle of the island. This earthy sand, mixed with equal parts of lime and of ashes (from the large, ancient midden near the farmhouse door), made a very cheap, strong mortar. With patience and practice I learned to build up the gaps in the walls first, and then, encouraged, went on to repair the roof. New rafters and plates were necessary in one place and here the driftwood timber was employed. I put in for a wall-plate a solid oak plank which should last at least a century. Laths were laid across the rafters, and I next gathered the fallen tiles and sorted them to their sizes, the largest at the eaves and smallest at the ridge. Each tile had to have a wooden peg to hang on to the laths by, and a bed of mortar to rest upon above the preceding row. It became a fascinating, if slow, task. But I was pleased because everything except the lime was produced on the island. Even the tiles had been dug from the little quarry on the island many years ago, and were very irregular, thick and heavy, but of a pleasant yellowy grey in colour.

CHAPTER VII

Lower Island Lodge

It had by this time become clear to me that I should need some shelter of my own on the mainland to which I could retire when forced to stay ashore during bad weather, instead of, as hitherto, burdening the hospitable farmer with an often unexpected guest. Therefore, the new year found me building a little hut on the bluebell slope above the haven, and where my boat rested when I was ashore.

Martinshaven is two miles away from the village, and from where I built the hut, overlooking the haven and the wide bay beyond, there was no house or farm visible. I was pleased to have the haven to myself, and I knew that a certain lady would not but be pleased too. Was not the bracken slope in front of the hut full of bluebells, foxgloves and lizards in summer? There was, too, a spring of water at the foot of the slope, and a pair of stonechats forever perched on the furze-and-bramble thicket above it. Therefore, while I worked there upon the hut, I was incredibly happy. John worked with me, and at intervals we voyaged down to the island to tend Richard and bring back rabbits.

We made this hut into two rooms, first digging into

the steep slope for a deep, secure foundation that would hold against all gales. One room was to be the living-room, and the other for storing goods. At midday, every day of the week, the post-boy brought me great treasure—a letter from the uncrowned queen of the island. When Thoreau was building his hut he read the newspaper his lunch was wrapped in. Surely it was a great pity that he had none such as I had to write his news for him.

Sometimes we stayed a few days on the island, carrying on with the work of converting the barn. John now worked all the time with me. He proved to be a clever mason, though he had not done such work before, and I now foresaw we should ourselves be able to do all the work on the island.

Early in February the mainland hut was finally lined and completed, and duly named, perhaps a little facetiously in view of its size, 'Lower Island Lodge'. Now I was free to turn my whole attention to the island buildings, but, happy in that, when forced to stay ashore I had my own roof under which to shelter.

The work on the barn now occupied so much of my time that I could ill spare any for the necessary routine of cooking meals and house-cleaning; nor could I spare John from his work. But my luck still stood, for I now received a letter from my one-time farm assistant, Henry, a boy of sixteen. He was out of work, and he wrote to ask if I could fulfil a hope I had once given him of employing him on the island. Henry was a nice young lad, much given to reading pirate and adventure stories, and he had, I believe, a very picturesque idea of what life on an island in the High Seas was like; so

I gave him the necessary instructions for getting down to Marloes and joining me.

February was a month of fairly quiet weather. The winter gales and rough seas gave way to cold easterly winds, with frost on the mainland but rarely on the island. At the beginning of the month we had had one bad crossing: the last of the gales taking us suddenly aback as we were entering Jack Sound en route for the mainland. Before we could run the sail down in order to reef it the wind-pressure snapped the yard in twain, and, a moment later, as the boat bumped over a high wave, the mast was jerked out of its step, so that mast, sail and broken yard all went by the board; the mast splitting a thwart in two at the same time through being unstepped and the consequent pressure on the clamp. With difficulty we saved the precious sail and mast, hauling it inboard again by the halyards, which were still fastened in the cleats. We then drifted through the Sound before the wind, pulling with the oars until we gained shelter and relief behind the Haze Point.

Spring was now coming rapidly to the island. In January frogs had spawned in my two ponds, and now, in February, the shearwaters were returning to the rabbit-burrows, for they began their absurd calling and cooing in the middle of the month. The herring-gulls now sat two by two sedately on the cliffs all around the island, evidently paired off and waiting for summer and the nesting-time. The great black-backed gulls called amorously and wheeled and circled endlessly above the island. They had never deserted us, even in stormy mid-winter. The 'sea-pies,' as John called the oyster-catchers, now invaded the meadows in couples, and made day and night merry with their 'ki-ki-ki-kivi-kivi-kivi' ad infinitum. The lapwings behaved in mad and merry fashion as they flew erratically over their breeding-ground on the island-bog. Larks and pipits sang airily on sunny days, and, in the garden, now dug from end to end, blackbirds and hedge-sparrows sang tunefully. Primroses and lesser celandines were opening out, and South Haven gave promise of being a carpet of flowers once more.

Lintels had to be put in the walls of the barn to take the four windows and the door. So we pierced the walls, which were two feet thick, very carefully, and inserted heavy lintels cut from driftwood planks. Then windows and door were duly placed and built in, making the barn light and warm.

It now remained to build the fireplace and chimney shaft. But while we were engaged on the foundation of this a fresh adventure was sprung upon us.

CHAPTER VIII

The Wreck of the Alice Williams

Many are the tales of wrecks on this coast. The Lower Island has had its share of them in the past, when ships were made of wood and did not sink easily, but more often drifted ashore on some unfriendly coast. Indeed the men of Marloes complain that they do not have a wreck on the coast now more than once in a decade, because modern-built ships sink on the spot. There is a legend that Skokholm is ringed around with wrecked vessels lying a few fathoms deep, and that is the reason why, so the folk say, there is now a lighthouse on the island.

Howbeit, one morning late in February, I strolled out-of-doors, early and eager to work, there to find, fast in the rocky cliff below tall Spy Rock, a fine old wooden schooner with all her sails spread to the now gentle south-east breeze! There had been a strong breeze all night, accompanied by heavy mist, and now here she was—a wonderful prize.

When you have lived long enough (it need not be very long!) on a sea-coast, everything that the sea gives up you grow greedy to take. You even dream of a great ship crushed on the beach, pouring out its life-blood of innumerable spars, bars, tools and treasure, which you will be greedy to fight for, steal, and hide from the sight of preventive officers. You think rather less of the possible loss of life than of the spoils of the wreck. In short, a wreck proves to you how avaricious you really are. I believe my first thoughts when I saw the schooner were as discreditable as any confirmed beachcomber's.

Looking directly down upon the schooner from the high cliff above I was able to admire her to my heart's content. The tops of her topmasts were on a level with me. Her two large sails, the main and fore, were all set, as were her two topsails, the upper and lower, on the foremast. Her bowsprit, in striking the cliffs, had broken off short, the stump leaning out over the lower cliff in such a way as to form a convenient gangway for agile persons. The jibsails, or headsails, were torn to shreds, which hung in the stay-wires of the broken bowsprit. The ship itself was quite fast in a cleft in the cliff. She had evidently blown in at high water, ramming her stern against the sheer cliff on one side, and her bow against the shelving rocks of the other side.

The decks were in confusion when John and I boarded her. Ropes and chains were strewn everywhere, but there was no sign of life aboard, only the gentle swaying of the sail-yards and booms in the breeze that could no longer move the fastened ship. The sea washed in and out of the below-decks of the cabin, the hold and the fo'c'sle.

A peep into the hold revealed the cargo. Instead of gold and silver ingots, as almost hoped for but not expected in these degenerate days, the hold was full of black diamonds—coal! There must have been two hundred tons of coal on board the good old *Alice Williams*, for that was her name, painted and carved on bow and stern.

When I looked over the bulwarks down into the now almost calm sea I saw much wooden wreckage floating close to the ship's side. The enormous rudder, torn out of its seat, was half afloat and half sunk by the weight of the iron fastenings on it.

Then quite suddenly I saw amid the wreckage a woman's face—a strong, bright face with piercing blue eyes that gazed far-seeing into the blue sky. The woman still wore her hair neatly coiled, with a black ribbon and red roses still twined in it. She also wore a white frock with an old-fashioned tight bodice, and around her neck was a rosary of jet and a black cross that matched her raven hair. She floated serenely on the water, despite the fact that one of her arms was missing.

'Quick, John,' I cried—'a rope here, boy!'

Again and again we threw a rope with a hook on the end down to the floating lady. She took not the slightest notice of our frantic efforts for her rescue. At last the grapple caught in a coil of her hair and without any ceremony we hauled her up bodily over the ship's rail. It was Alice Williams herself, the serene and lovely figure-head of the schooner, dressed, as she was first conceived, in the fashion of the eighteen-fifties. True to her ship she had stayed to the last, even when struck off by the rocks, and when all the others had abandoned it.

We propped her up beside the ship's wheel on the poop, and I then paced the decks wondering what to do with this prize ship. Would she move out of her rocky berth? I could but try.

'Stand by there, John, my lad!' I bellowed, taking the wheel from Alice. 'Cut anchors and hoist the flying jib; we'll away to London Town and sell this good ship for a thousand golden doubloons!'

'Aye, aye, sir!' cried John, who in his day had served on more than one schooner and ketch. 'Hey there, bos'n, fetch the crew and step lively to it! Up aloft wi' ye and shake out the foretop skysails!'

The gulls laughed back at us, and the high cliff echoed, but the ship never moved. She was in her last haven. Her wooden sides and keel had settled once and for all in the cradle of red island boulders. The wheel-shaft had broken off near the rudder-post, and there was a hole in her bows from which coal already leaked.

'Ye'd best make the most of her, sir,' said John. 'In a day of wind she'll be swept to the bottom.'

''Tis plunder then, John,' I said. 'We'll save what we can.'

Below deck, as the tide ebbed, we found the cabin, fo'c'sle, and sail-room in great disorder and full of broken panelling, planks and timber. The captain's instruments, the ship's china and kitchenware were all washed away already, but I saw my opportunity to lay in a stock of coal to last me for many years. It remained to get together enough hands to work the cargo out of the hold and on to the ledges of the cliff—no easy task I was to find.

That day John and I lowered the brand-new mainsail and the old red foresail and cut them from the bolt-ropes. On the end of the lower topsail-yard which leaned out towards the cliff, we fixed a block, and through it reeved a rope to the ship's winch. John turned the winch while I fastened the sails one at a time on to the rope. Up and up soared the folded mainsail until it touched the block on the end of the yard and, hanging thus over the cliff and the ship, could go no higher. Then I climbed ashore, and as John lowered the rope slowly pulled the great heavy canvas down on to the cliff. In this way the foresail was hoisted ashore, and finally Alice Williams herself was tenderly swung up to the yard and down to the cliff. There I leaned her against the rocks in such a position that she could watch all subsequent proceedings on her wrecked home.

CHAPTER IX

Henry Samples the High Seas

As Henry was expected at Marloes the next day we went ashore to fetch him. I also took the opportunity to ring up the local ships' underwriter in order to put my salvage operations on a legal footing, a necessary proceeding even on a remote island.

From the underwriter I learned that the *Alice Williams* had got out of control in the night, her headsails having been carried away by the half-gale, and, as she was in danger of drifting on to the rocks in this unmanageable state, anchors were dropped. These, however, dragged, so, after sending up distress flares, the crew of five finally lowered the ship's boat and abandoned the schooner. They were later picked up by a trawler near St Ann's and taken to Milford Haven.

Henry was mightily excited about the wreck and impatient to see the island. Richard had now finished his catching for the season, so we had brought him ashore, and now took Henry back in his stead. There was also a lorry load of slates, lime and other gear, for the rebuilding of the island dwelling, waiting shipment to Martinshaven. I decided, therefore, to load up the *Foxtrot* and to sail down in her instead of using the *Storm-Petrel*.

A stiff south-east wind was blowing when we put out for Jack Sound, and we were deeply loaded with over a ton of material. In addition I had put on board the handwinch I usually kept on the mainland beach for hauling up my boat, as I thought it might be useful to use, in partnership with schooner's winch, in salvage work. But, in spite of such a steadying load for our sail below Jack Sound, the wind increased to such an extent that we could not beat down to the island, even with a strong tide in our favour. Henry's first crossing was therefore to be an exciting one; an introduction to the island for him to remember long afterwards.

Almost before we realized our danger the wind began to strengthen still more. A squall of rain helped this increase, and we began to blow out of the helpful current into slack water under the lee shore of Skomer. It was too late to run back through Jack Sound, for we could not fetch there, and in a very few minutes we expected to be wrecked ourselves on the wind-tossed sea beating on Skomer's rocks. Poor Henry, now alarmed in addition to being very sick, crouched helplessly in the midst of the cargo. John held to the tiller, trying desperately to manoeuvre the *Foxtrot* into Jack Sound, while I pulled an oar to help whenever the lurching boat allowed me to dip one.

One chance seemed to be left to us; to try to run up through the Little Sound between Skomer and Midland against the tide. By so doing there was just a chance of escaping from the south-east gale, saving ourselves and incidentally the boat and cargo. The current in Little Sound is notorious for its strength at any time, and to-day marked the top of the spring tides.

We entered the narrow neck of this sound at a moment when the ebb current was at its strongest; actually at low water, when the seas roared down southward to meet the blast of the wind in direct opposition, so raising a tumultous barrier of broken water. Into this white smother the *Foxtrot* plunged willy-nilly, driven before the rising gale.

It was now a contest between tide and wind. The current hurried us southward, the wind blew us northward; the sea merely tossed us about unmercifully, and dashed water inboard at every motion. John held grimly to the tiller, skilfully keeping the boat head on to the current and the breaking water. When we reached the strongest part of the tide we also reached the point where the wind was strongest, and that was at the narrowest part of the Little Sound. Nevertheless, the wind was not strong enough to enable us to beat the tide; one neutralized the other, and we were, to all appearances, anchored under full sail in a roaring torrent.

How long could we keep the boat head-on to the rough water? One misguided touch of the tiller might slew the boat round broadside on and then all would be over. Again, it would not be very long before the spray would about fill the boat, and then one big wave would settle the matter by sinking us. Worse still, the current was not due to slack for at least another two hours.

When I saw we were not making headway through, I scrambled forward and again began using an oar to help, and it was the maddest rowing I have ever put hand to. At one moment the oar would be half-buried in a rising wave, at the next waving fruitlessly in the air. Yet the little extra pull, when I was able to make it, gradually helped us against the roaring tide, so I sat with my back against the mast and pulled heartily.

Only a little later, however, the blade of the oar was drawn down very suddenly by a high wave. I strove to slip it out of the water by twisting the oar until the blade was on edge, but was not quick enough. The handle, forced by the pressure on the blade, came up against my chest, my back being already against the mast. Something was bound to give way, and a second later the oar obliged, for it snapped in two at the rowlock. We then began to lose way and drift down the Little Sound again.

John had cried from his boatman's heart a desperate 'Ah!' as he saw his prized eighteen-foot oar snap and go by the board, and he looked at me dubiously as I took up a heavy, fourteen-foot one. However, it was necessary to get out of the smother before we were swamped, and he himself dare not leave the tiller for one second.

I used the utmost caution with this second oar and gradually helped to work the *Foxtrot* out of the seething tide-race. Then, just as I had relaxed my efforts, a little exhausted, the oar was again trapped suddenly by a wave, I was pinned against the mast by the handle, and at once snap! went the heavy oar. There was now but one oar left to us, a pretty predicament should we be forced to row, as, indeed, we soon had to.

We were now clear of the worst tide and were safely in the shelter of the Skomer north cliffs, but to get back to the mainland was our next problem. It would mean a stiff row along under the cliffs and across the smooth upper side of Jack Sound to Martinshaven—but with only one oar.

Any port in a storm is a true saying. We could not row with but one oar, so we sailed on into the north haven of Skomer, that calm and spacious harbourage, sailed right on to the landing beach. I then jumped out, ran to the boat belonging to the island resident, and, as there was no one in sight to beg or borrow from, took one of the four oars lying on the beach beside the boat. With this oar to match that last one in the *Foxtrot* we at last succeeded, after two hours of weary pulling, in reaching Martinshaven.

Poor Henry, huddled all the while in the stern, wet, sick and bedraggled, was helped ashore, the cargo unloaded and the boat hauled up. And as if to mock at our plight the storm passed away shortly afterwards.

CHAPTER X

Alice Signs her Last Crew

The next day was marvellously calm, and I was early astir seeking oars to replace the pair I had broken. I was recommended to a certain master mariner, owner of a coasting ketch, and on visiting him at his home at Sandy Haven was courteously given a spare pair of oars.

Sandy Haven lies within the shelter of St Ann's Head and the calm waters of Milford Haven. Calm, then, are the waters of Sandy Haven, and free from the surge of the Atlantic. Trees fringe the tide-line on each side of the inlet, and rarely does the gale shake the tall tops of the beeches which the high land shelters so securely. Captain Cristal's ketch lay moored against the little quay on which his house abutted, the whole forming a charming picture in this very charming, wooded inlet.

The spirit of adventure seized Captain Cristal when he learned of the wreck of the *Alice Williams*.

'I'll come with you and help save all that coal. It's a windfall for you. There might be some useful ropes and gear there, too, to suit the old ketch, she needs them sorely. I'll come along with you now.'

And so saying he did come. He packed a kitbag and

roused out a second hand, a jobbing labourer, to come with him. At Marloes we picked up John and Henry, and, strange to say, the mason whom hitherto I had been unable to induce to come and repair the island house. The wreck proved a better lure to the mason, and in addition I promised him a boatload of coal for his services, for I was glad to have him to help us. So, at the last moment, there was an assembly of six on the beach at Martinshaven: Captain Cristal and Billy his man; the mason and John; Henry and myself.

Alice Williams had weathered the storm of yesterday easily, for it had come and gone at low water, while the sea had ebbed quite away from her; on arrival, and when all the newcomers had admired the wreck and trod the decks till the novelty of doing so had worn off, we set to work, and carried on merrily for several days. John and the mason wound the winch which hoisted the coal out of the hold by the basket-load. Cristal and Billy loaded the baskets while I pulled them in to the cliff and piled the coal on the ledges. It was very heavy, hard work. On the third day Cristal missed his footing on the deck and fell into the hold. Luckily the tide had just begun to fill the ship, so that he had nothing more hurtful then a swim amid the half-awash cargo, but, until he emerged, black and wet, we were mystified by his sudden and complete disappearance. Even this fall did not damp his merry spirits, which were at all times the life of this strangely assorted crew.

Henry, a delighted grin perpetually on his fresh young face, helped, in between his duties, as head cook and bottle-washer. When we were thirsty between meals he brought us an enormous kettle (ex *Alice Williams*) of tea. He was detailed to get our supper, which consisted of a saucepan or two full of boiled potatoes, swedes and salt beef ('ship's junk' from the pickle-chest of the *Alice Williams*)—a simple enough supper, but one to which our ravenous appetites did full justice.

Henry, as a matter of fact, was living a life highly to his taste. He had stepped from prosaic farm-life into High Adventure mid island, sea, and wreck. He gazed at first in awe at the stranded schooner, treading the decks circumspectly and looking giddily up at her tall masts.

'Do you think I could climb the rigging?' he asked on the first day, as he watched the experienced John run up to the crow's nest like the proverbial cat, adjust some ropes in the masthead blocks, and presently come sliding down on a hand-rope at a reckless pace.

'Up with you, lad. Tumble to it!' I replied, and up he went, very gingerly and not very far the first time.

After supper in the old house the six of us would gather before a roaring fire of new coal from the wreck, and yarns flew around until midnight. Captain Cristal had an inexhaustible supply of personal adventures and anecdotes, while the mason ran him a close second and tried to out-talk him. Cristal led the laughter at the end of each of his yarns and compelled us all to join in, if only because the heartiness of his laugh amused us. Henry gaped through each yarn, and then laughed so immoderately that Cristal would turn to him with an enormous smile and say 'Good heavens, boy! What's the joke?' and thus set Henry off into hysterics.

When we were all too tired to talk we fell asleep. Henry and I shared my little room; John and Billy slept on some hay on the floor; the mason and Cristal shared the big driftwood four-poster, and all night long grumbled and quarrelled over territory upon it.

Some time before dawn the energetic Cristal would relinquish his share of the bed, to the profound relief of the mason, who was now able to snore in peace, and stir up the dying fire. This was the signal for a general uprising. When breakfast, consisting of the inevitable bacon, bread and butter, and tea, was ready, the mason put his boots on and joined us. Thus the day's work began somewhere about sunrise, and went on until sunset.

The sea, at high water, was on a level with the schooner's deck, and it was not possible to work then for an hour or two, so we spent this period in hauling the coal, sails, rope and gear already ashore on to higher ground, using my handwinch, which was mounted on the top of the cliff.

Each tide had its effect on the *Alice Williams*, working and prying loose more and more of her planking. Soon the keel was pressing up through the ship, each day lifting the masts a few inches higher above the sinking deck. At high-water the whole ship rocked gently to and fro, the masts swaying and creaking rather ominously. The first breeze or groundswell must inevitably bring her total dissolution. Therefore, we toiled each day until we were worn out, trying to save the coal that at each tide leaked by the ton out of the rent in the bows. But after four days' work we had piled up enough coal, I hoped, to last me many years.

We began to strip the decks as soon as the rising tide made work dangerous in the hold. First the cook's galley, a little deck-house not more than six feet square, was unshipped and bodily chained for removal. The winch slowly wound this shanty up to the yard-arm just like any basket of coal, and we had the unique sight of a cook's galley dangling fifty feet up on the topsail yard. Then the other winch slowly pulled it in to the cliff, while all below hid their heads in anticipation of something giving way.

In this manner, too, the main topmast of the schooner was unshipped and hauled ashore, for I had my eye on this for a flagstaff.

The tiny wheelhouse was deemed too heavy to lift to the yard-arm; it was therefore thrown overboard and towed by boat around to South Haven, where it was finally rolled up the broad landing-steps to a safe place on the grass. Cristal secured for his ketch heavy mooring and towing ropes, some gaffs, booms and other useful items.

At the end of six days most of the coal had been washed out of the hold, and the old schooner was tilted at a sharp angle, waiting for her end. The masts were askew and only held in place by the stout rigging. I believe there were tears in Alice's eyes, but to spare her the final agonies I carried her up to the top of Spy Rock beside the island flagpole. Here she might still breast a salty wind and look out over restless seas, with foam and white water below her.

It was now getting too risky to work on board. The neap tides did not entirely leave the schooner by day. Moreover, my crew were thoroughly exhausted, ready to give up and depart to civilization once more. So we put them ashore, with due thanks for their voluntary services, and two days later there came a half gale from south-east and the *Alice Williams* was totally destroyed. The wind and sea piled her fragments high on the island beaches, and I was able to select all and more than I wanted of oak beams and other timber for the reconstruction of my future home. (Good value indeed for five pounds—the token price I paid the underwriter for the *Alice Williams*. As a wreck she was of course of no value to a mainland man.)

CHAPTER XI

The Wheelhouse

With March birds flocked in still greater numbers to the island, the early spring arrivals mingling with the winter visitors. In the middle of the month the wheatears arrived, dozens of them flying low about the stone hedgewalls, bobbing, curtseying and calling 'Jack, Jack,' to me. The lesser black-backed gulls came quite suddenly to occupy the island bog. They sat together in pairs on the long grass, and resented with loud cries the approach of any human form. The ravens had long built their nest on the cliff in Mad Bay, and now had a ravenous young brood of five to feed. They had built a strong nest of dead heather-stems and roots, and had lined it warmly with fibres and rabbits'-wool. Late in the month came the chiffchaff, and flights of starlings, rooks and chaffinches; all transitory visitors, hurrying in some northerly direction to their breeding haunts.

Primroses were at their best, growing in all the bays and on the slopes of the island cliffs. South Haven was yellow with primroses and lesser celandines. Sea campion and violets were just beginning to flower.

While we were occupied in building the barn my thoughts turned much on the future. This first year I would not have time to be a fisherman; the summer would pass all too quickly in house-building. Yet it was all very well to build a home and then not have the means to support one. I therefore planned out my slender capital as carefully as I could. In the future my income must come from the products of the island; from rabbits, fish and the future farm. To produce most of my foodstuffs was the ideal to aim at, and to achieve as much independence as possible. The garden must be a large one. I must keep goats for milk and hens for eggs. Later I would be a shepherd as well, with a large flock of sheep to give both pleasure and profit.

I had already bought a young nanny goat, a pretty creature with a light fawn coat, white feet below the knees, and face and ears daintily marked with white. This was Katherine, or Kitty for short; she was not expected to come into milking profit until next spring. Now I also obtained a young goat already in milk, naming her Matilda or Matty for short. Finally there was a young billy-goat to form the nucleus of the small flock of three or four milking-goats which we would eventually content ourselves with. Matilda was of a darker fawn colour than Katherine, and Rufus, the billy, was of the colour that his own name implied.

Of chickens Doris had charge of the flock destined to lead an island life. They were Rhode Islanders, headed by Jonathan, a noble cockerel with an unimpeachable pedigree. There were favourable reports forwarded to me of the hatching and rearing of this feathered community.

As to the garden, this had already been deeply dug

over, and now waited to be set. Doris intended to come and set the garden seeds herself, but I was not sure that I wanted her to come just yet, and to find nothing accomplished in house-restoration.

We now worked feverishly at the barn; Henry took entire charge of the culinary and house-cleaning operations in the old dwelling. I taught him how to make bread and to cook generally, and he was soon adding flourishes of his own to the art. He read recipes secretly and brought some amazing, but mostly very palatable, dishes to the table. The fare was simple enough. Fried bread and bacon for breakfast; vegetables, mostly swedes and potatoes for dinner, with bully beef or some tinned meat of some kind; for tea, toast, butter and jam, and on Sundays any cake Henry thought fit to surprise us with. At each meal mugs of tea helped to allay a thirst obtained by hard work. Just before bedtime, cocoa and toast was to be had by anyone who liked to get it himself. Sundays were holidays. Once a week, and sometimes once only in a fortnight, did we cross to the mainland for letters and more building material.

Beyond slates for the house-roof, and lime for mortar, we had little heavy material to carry. New windows had to be made to order at a joinery, but the doors I built myself.

We had an excellent supply of oak from the wreck for lintels and beams. The brass-bound wheel of the schooner we fixed in the breast of the chimney-piece we had built in the barn. When this wheel was duly polished until the wood and brass shone it was quite a resplendent sight under the lofty beams of this large room. Moreover, it was not to be a mere ornament. If one seized the spokes and swung the wheel four turns to starboard a chain came sliding down the chimney. It was an easy matter then to hook the kettle on for tea. When the kettle boiled, four turns of the wheel to port raised it off the fire. This was the great trick to play on visitors. Henry would nonchalantly swing the great wheel and be intensely delighted to see the stranger momentarily mystified by the action of the kettle.

Early in April the barn was as far renovated as I intended it to be for the present, and we moved in wholesale from the house. My few items of furniture were easily accommodated by the roomy barn. We laid the great red foresail of the schooner over the floor, which was composed of wide, flat slabs of red island stone. The ship's tattered flags, her lifebuoys and some panelling, decorated and made bright the whitewashed walls. Opposite the wheel and chimney, at the other end of the room, we fixed the heavy, carved timber, decorated in white and black check, which once accompanied Alice on the schooner's bow. Above it, in the high, apex window, the ship's binnacle and compass rested: to port and starboard respectively, in the corners of this end of the room, hung the ship's red port lamp and her green starboard one. Outside the door the ship's fog-bell served as a musical knocker for visitors and a summons-bell for meals, whilst her carved name-plate, torn from her bow by the sea, had been rescued and was now nailed forever on a conspicuous lower beam inside.

It was in this picturesque den that we lived while

we were repairing the dwelling-home. We slept each on his own ship's cot, rescued from the wreck and newly sewn over with red sail canvas; and very comfortably we slept too. Barn was a much too prosaic name for this living-room, dominated by the dazzling brightness of the brass on the wheel, which Henry was under strict orders to keep shining. So henceforth it was called the 'Wheelhouse.'

CHAPTER XII

A Natural Cinema

When Doris came in April to plant her garden, Admiral—who, by the way, in case you have not already guessed this, is her father—came with her. We had whitewashed and decorated the one habitable little room in the old house for the distinguished lady visitor. For the first time also the table was spread in state in the Wheelhouse, a genuine tablecloth and china making a spotless display such as the old place had never known before. This, with a roaring fire of wreck coal and wood, was to welcome and warm the visitors after their cold voyage over a wind-whipped sea.

Zealously did Doris sow the garden with beans, peas, carrots, parsnips, and plant greens, rhubarb, shallots, currants and gooseberries, while I laid in the potato rows. Admiral, with his expert mastery of the joiner's craft was not idle either. Together the three of us demolished the partition between the house kitchen and the roofless room beside it, in order to work the will of Doris to have a larger kitchen. This partition proved to be nearly three feet thick and contained a chimney and fireplace which had been walled in at some time long past. The result was that, when all the stones and mortar had been removed, Doris had a long, low-roofed kitchen for her delight, facing southwards to the shelter of the hill.

Those few days passed all too quickly, and then we were left alone once more. John and I now gave all our attention to the house, working steadily all day until five o'clock, when Henry would summon us to tea. After tea Henry and John were free to enjoy themselves in the simple delights of sailing and fishing about the island in the *Storm-Petrel*. John initiated Henry into the mysteries of lobster-pot-making, and the results were not without profit to the island bill-of-fare. In turn we had lobster, crab, pollack, and later on mackerel to vary the bully-beef menu.

The spring weather turned out to be ideal. For the whole month northerly winds prevailed, making the sea so calm in South Haven that the *Storm-Petrel* was moored day and night on the tranquil water there.

The puffins returned late in March to the Sounds, and there was great excitement on the 3rd of April, when they finally made up their minds to land. This they did very suddenly and thoroughly at midday, flying inland by the hundred and occupying all their favourite positions on the high points, the rock outcrops and the stony hedgewalls. There they jigged and bowed and laughed sonorously in their usual manner, for three hours, before betaking themselves away en masse. Two days later they again made a landing in force, and, as before, disappearing after a few hours. A bitter north-east wind, on April 16th, had the effect of driving them entirely away from the sea near the island, but they returned in thousands on the 18th, and the next day landed for the season.

The shearwaters, of course, had been here since February, and were now about to lay their solitary, white egg in the recess at the end of a rabbit-burrow. The storm-petrels had only begun to arrive at night in the last few days of April.

April and May were, indeed, wonderful months for one who loved birds. Each day saw new visitors, quickly come and quickly gone. After the wheatears and chiffchaffs came the swallows and sand-martins. Every day throughout April, May and early June swallows passed over the meadows, sometimes in hundreds, but more often by two's and three's, steadily from dawn until dusk. Then came willow-wrens, swarming in the newly-grown nettles and bramble-bushes, olivaceous-coloured birds difficult to distinguish from the chiffchaffs at a distance, except when, at rare intervals, they paused to utter a few bars of song. But all these migrants were, as a rule; too restless and busy seeking food to have inclination to sing.

White wagtails on their way north, probably to Iceland and the Faroes, visited the island from March to mid-April, generally in small flocks of from a dozen to fifty. They came freely about the garden and buildings, causing a certain excitement to the pair of pied wagtails, their close relations, who had built a nest in an old wall near the Wheelhouse.

A few cuckoos called over the island, but were soon gone. Whitethroats were plentiful on some days, and late in April came the sleek, brown sedge-warblers, swarming in the nettles as did the willow-wrens. One pair remained to nest in the thicket of hemlock drop-wort at the foot of the home meadow, where a spring runs down from the well. The male bird was the sweetest songster we had on the island that summer, and after singing all day would begin again at night as soon as the first incoming shearwater's cry disturbed his fitful sleep.

A few swifts, a few house-martins, and many whinchats completed the list of April migrants. With May came spotted flycatchers, grasshopper-warblers and turtle-doves. Of larger birds there were occasional rooks, daws, common sandpipers and whimbrel, besides quite a long list of birds of which only one or two of its kind were noted.

After tea in the Wheelhouse it was our common practice to stand awhile at the windows looking out on the meadow. At this hour, after the quietness of teatime and the cessation of the noise of building operations, the wild rabbits came out of their burrows to feed. They grazed and gambolled within a few yards of the Wheelhouse windows. Soon we learned to recognize individuals by certain peculiarities; for instance one was particularly fat and large, another thin and lanky, one completely black, another with a white mark on its face, and one with its tail carried on one side, or, as John called it, 'hard-to-port.' It was amusing to watch the antics, flirtations, and mimic battles of the bunnies. 'Hard-to-port' was a redoubtable warrior, and could perform the highest leap over an opponent's head. Rarely did rivals come to grips and lie scramming each other on the grass. They preferred to kick each other in passing and leaping and dancing around each other. The does tranquilly engaged in grazing all the time, their little ones darting timidly in and out of the burrows to snatch a bite of grass at intervals.

When a buzzard passed overhead there was a general crouching down, with ears laid flat. The little rabbits fled underground. The wicked black-backed gulls would walk about unconcernedly among the rabbits, and with the greatest cunning and affected indifference would edge closer and closer to a family group. At last, when near enough, the sharp, heavy beak would strike a young rabbit, there would be a pitiful scream, and away the gull would fly with its stricken victim in its mouth. These gulls fed largely on baby rabbits thus taken by stealth, and the greater black-backs even slew puffins by patiently waiting at the mouths of the burrows for Mr Puffin to come out.

The windows framed pictures of the small birds too. A pair of wheatears nested deep in a crevice in a bank opposite, and all day long carried grubs and flies to their hungry young. Spotted flycatchers, cuckoos and turtle doves perched on the bank at times, all welcome if momentary spring visitors. One day a very handsome and distinguished visitor settled on the bank in front of the window. It was a hoopoe, a brilliantly coloured bird not unlike a small jay, with a sulphur-tipped, fan-shaped crest on its head which it erected for a moment as it settled on the hedge-bank. The hoopoe is a rare British bird, and this pretty fellow did not stay with us longer than one day. It flew about the island with that rising and falling method of flight, wings now half-closed and now wide-spread, adopted by jay and woodpecker.

Nearly all the visitors and non-breeding birds had

left by the end of May. It was clear that the starlings did not intend to stay and nest in the summer. The flocks gradually dwindled until but one pair was left, and even these two, after a thorough inspection of the old buildings, thought it best to fly away in the end.

I had never seen an ordinary house-sparrow on the island until one day late in April a solitary cock arrived, worn out as if through the fatigue of a long flight. For two days it was too weak to chirp, but, presently, fattening on our table-crumbs, it began to call incessantly. Of course there was no response—the nearest sparrows I knew of lived at Marloes—and at last Mr Sparrow flew away, no doubt despairing of colonizing this lonely isle.

CHAPTER XIII

House Building

With what zeal did I attack the old dwelling-house. The whole roof came off, almost to the last rafter and beam, so rotten and worm-eaten did we find the timbers. This work occupied our attention first, the intention being to put the roof on so that we could have a dry place to work under. Here the timbers from the wreck provided us with the necessary replacements; with wall-plates, collars, main beams and rafters, mostly of old oak and pine. The few remaining Welsh-dug slates were taken off, and when the whole roof had been retimbered I began putting on ordinary modern pale-grey slates, which, at a distance and from the mainland, give the appearance of a pure, white roof, in keeping with the white-washed walls of house and buildings. The roof was a fine vantage-point, and as I worked I could survey my little kingdom, the countless thousands of my feathered subjects, and admire the acres of bluebells and thrift. The weather, as I have said, was exceedingly kind to us, and had I but known the haste to get the roof done first of all would not have been necessary, for we had no rain to speak of.

All the windows had to be renewed, and, except

where they were of stone, new lintels put in above them. The two fireplaces also required lintels. Fortunately among the timbers rescued from the *Alice Williams* were a number of heavy oak beams, eight inches square, which had come from the captain's cabin and were in consequence nicely planed and finished. These I used for lintels and main supports. It was curious and interesting to discover that the old lintel, charred and almost immemorial which I removed from the kitchen fireplace, was also a timber from a wooden sailing-ship. In fact, it was of exactly the same width and thickness, and had the same finishing lines as the timber I replaced it with. I was therefore repeating the history of the building of this house, and this charred lintel could not have come from an oak tree felled less than four hundred years ago.

The whole of the inside and outside walls of the house needed replastering and at this work John proved himself very capable. The sandpit was dug deeply for a fine earth, the midden-heap was sifted for the last ashes, and lime was added until we had a great mound of mortar for the purpose. The walls were scraped of loose plaster and earth and the work began. In this way most of the mason-work fell to John, the carpentry to me.

New floors were required in all the rooms except the pantry and porch, where we left the red island flagstones as we found them. The wreck could not provide us with boards suitable for flooring, and we had to import these, as also the boards for door-making. The doors I made, in my amateurish way, very plainly of straight boards and fixed lift-up latches to them. There would be no need for locks and keys in my home.

Another thing pleased me, I had no need to be too particular with my building operations; the house was already so quaintly built 'after a whimsical manner,' as Fenton, in his *Tour through Pembrokeshire* remarks, that my own improvements and unconventional methods could not but be somewhat in keeping with the inimitable style of the whole. Not one doorway, for instance, matched another: some are high and wide, some low, some narrow, and some high and narrow. The windows vary in the same manner.

The floor of the kitchen I put down in concrete, a range was imported, one specially suitable for bread-baking; the walls were plastered and white-washed, and the first room was at last finished. Next, the pantry was fitted with a new, north-facing window and with shelves, the walls white-washed and the red flags scrubbed until they were a true red again. The guestroom was refloored with flooring boards laid over joists consisting of the thick deck-planks of the *Alice Williams*. The main-room, when the ante-room partition had been knocked down and a new floor put across the timbers of the loft overhead, made an attractively large living-room. The long, oak beams, cleaned of ages of dirt, were still straight and strong, so that we were saved the trouble of tearing the walls down to renew them. For a stairway to the loft we had the step-ladder from the cabin of the wreck. The handrail from the schooner, too, when trimmed to required lengths, furnished me with the framing of the fireplace, which I had made rather spacious for burning logs and driftwood.

Alice Williams, you will now see, had been most useful, saving much expense of material and the labour of ferrying it over. She had furnished me with timbers of such quality as I should scarcely have been able to afford. But I must not forget that, apart from the house-building, there were other directions in which she had been equally useful. There were, for instance, innumerable items of use in boating, such as canvas, rope, wire, blocks, chains, tools, etc. Her fresh-water tank, capable of holding 200 gallons, we set up for catching and storing precious rain-water from the house-roof. The cook's galley we rolled laboriously across the meadows into one of the farm folds, and there I set it up to serve as a fowl-house when Jonathan & Co. arrived. The other deck-house was similarly rolled into a convenient place near the house.

Shortly after arriving on the island—the winter before—I had erected a short flagstaff on Spy Rock, one of the highest points on the island. Whenever we crossed to the mainland we ran up a flag (the Welsh dragon be it remarked) to warn the rabbit-dealer that we were coming over with a cargo for him. Now, in the summer, we used the flag to announce our crossing to anyone who might be waiting to meet us at Martinshaven. The flag-pole, however, was but a small one, merely an item that had drifted ashore on the island one day, and now that I had the tall topmast of the schooner I set about substituting this. Because of the convenience of having it near the house the topmast was erected on the 'Mountain,' as we facetiously called the protecting hillock behind the house. The Mountain is of a lower altitude than Spy Rock, but the extra height of the topmast made up for this.

Later, when the Welsh dragon had been torn to shreds by degrees in the perpetual breezes, Doris made a special flag for the island. How pleased were we when we first hoisted the new flag on the newly painted white topmast. There, spread to the breeze on a field of green, bordered alternately black and white, danced three storm-petrels, black with white rumps, flying towards the mast. The fluttering of the two tails of the long flag helped to create this illusion of actual flight. It was a masterpiece, this flag of ours.

The gulls had long finished laying by now. No longer could Henry, who had developed a passion for their eggs fried in fat, collect them with safety. He had, however, put down a few hundred in pickle, which were to last him a few weeks at least. There were strict orders as to egg-collecting on the island. I allowed only the taking of eggs of the black-backed gulls, but of these in the season there had been more than enough for all of us. Nor did the collecting seem to interfere much with the number of young hatched by these gulls. They went on laying until the middle of June, at which time many were already hatched. In July the island bog was alive with young gulls.

For, incredible as it may seem, July did arrive, and found me putting the last touches to the interior of the home I had promised Doris, though there was much to be done still to the outside; a lot of pioneering still left for her to take part in.

CHAPTER XIV

Wedding-Day

July the twelfth proved a day of sunshine after many days of uncertain weather and mist. There was a slight breeze from the south-east, so that I was able to sail quietly northwards from the island, and across St Bride's Bay to St Bride's Haven. Here, within a stone's throw of the church, anchor was dropped and I went ashore to meet my bride.

St Bride's Church is prettily placed beside the sandy beach. There is no village nearby, its sole neighbours being only a few scattered farms and cottages, and on the hill to westward the high tower of St Bride's Castle.

When the ceremony was over, shortly after noon, our parents and sisters, almost the sole witnesses of our quiet wedding, drank our health at the feast held on the edge of the grass, after which we were free to sail away alone together. It was almost the first time I had handled the boat without John, but I was proud to be able to sail away in the bright, newly painted *Storm-Petrel* with my bride. Proudly did the infant engine start us on our way, and then, when I hoisted sail, we sped away out into St Bride's Bay with a hissing wake of white foam behind us.

First of all Doris must needs view the home built for her, and to this end we sailed down for the island. But when we had passed through Jack Sound we met a heavy mist rolling up from the Atlantic. Some farmers, aware of the wedding, had assembled on the cliff near Jack Sound and now fired us a salute from their double-barrels, and just before the mist enveloped us entirely.

The wind then dropped away, the sails flapped idly, and the mist thickened until we could see no more than a few yards before us. Some shearwaters, those mist and fog-loving birds, began to pass us in the Broad Sound, skimming without apparent effort, now showing their white breasts and now their black upperparts; first with the left wing-tip almost touching the sea and then the right wing-tip, in a movement that reminded us of the right and left swing of a skater.

As we drew closer to our island home, steering entirely by compass, the numbers of puffins, gulls, razorbills and guillemots resting on the water increased until we were soon forging through large flocks of birds. And so we sailed till at last we caught the faint, intermittent blast of the fog signal from the lighthouse: then the faint wash of sea upon rocks; and so in deep mist we entered the South Haven of our island home.

CHAPTER XV

Promised Lands

Among many of the Lands Promised to Doris Grassholm was first and foremost. We were to have a honeymoon on Grassholm; we were to be the first honeymooners on that lonely Atlantic isle. Long ago I had promised her this, in a valorous moment when all things seemed easy to achieve if she so wished. And now the wedding was over and the bride ready for the honeymoon. I therefore asked her to pray for a northerly wind if she still wished to sail there.

While the wind stayed in the south we sailed elsewhere, taking a fair breeze where it blew us. Thus, the day after the wedding found us sailing before a mild sou-wester on the calm waters of Milford Haven and that evening found us drifting with the tide in the wooded reaches of the Cleddau, listening to hooting owl and reeling night-jar.

The hoped-for wind came stealing out of the north two days later and found us at the port of Martinshaven, whither we had sailed the previous evening. The wind was true north and blowing steadily, the morning was full of sunshine, and our hearts full of morning happiness. 'To sea! To sea!' was the cry, 'Where e'er the wind will blow us!'

One by one the Marloes fishermen were putting out to sea, and presently, when we had scraped together all the provisions we could find, and filled a pannier with water, we set forth too. There was a merry 'altogether-heave-ho!' as we together launched our strong craft; then 'jump in and stand by with the boat-hook.' For the sea was breaking choppily on Martinshaven beach, the north wind blowing upon this north-facing beach, and a short pull-off with oars necessary ere the infant engine was set to work.

Northward we pointed her while we trimmed our vessel, making all snug and secure in case we encountered choppy seas. Then did I hoist sail; first the wide, white lug, then the white jib upon the improvised bowsprit. The *Storm-Petrel* sprang forward to their urge, pointing due west, and we sailed away north of Skomer for the far Isle of Grassholm crossing the north-streaming tide above Jack Sound and past the Garland Stone of Skomer.

Fishermen, bending their backs over oars and lobster-pots in the shelter of Skomer cliffs, must have seen the full beauty of the *Storm-Petrel* as she lay over to the brisk northerly breeze, sailing out to sea on the last of the northern stream. Her white freeboard danced merrily in harmony with the white-capped wavelets of tide and wind-whipped sea, her stern parted the water with an eager, smiting sound, and the song of her rushing, eddying wake soothed the uproar of the noisy Infant, as we called the boat's engine. The breeze was so good when we got out into the open sea beyond Skomer that we silenced the Infant and rushed on to the pleasant murmur of parting waves and sails close-filled with the favouring wind.

After all, the *Storm-Petrel* was but a small craft to be sailing Atlantic seas, and I must confess that, at first, I had qualms about all our voyages, and especially about adventuring across the tide-races to a harbourless islet.

The *Storm-Petrel* is but seventeen feet long by five and a half of beam, and carries a pocket engine of a strength equal to two men rowing. She is prettily painted in white with red lines, and when her two white sails are out on her white mast and Doris is at the tiller, am I content to sail in her forever. I care not for a bigger boat that needs a larger crew and more gear, and that cannot creep in and out of sounds and creeks, lie upon tiny beaches, or be hauled out of the water without extra hands. Commend me to a small boat for summer sailing, and one that has also an infant engine to do the hardest work. A small engine, too, has these advantages: it is simple to run, costs little to do so, and does not go too fast to spoil the pleasure of sailing; yet when the breeze is faint the engine will help drive the ship forward, creating more wind to help fill the idle sails.

The tall cliffs of Skomer slowly faded behind us and that faraway isle of ours—the red land of the Lower Island—and nearer and nearer loomed the green shore of Hy Brasail, famed, among other things, for its colony of gannets; for here dwells the only colony of these birds in all England and Wales. There are now but a few others in Scotland and Ireland, though formerly they bred on Lundy Island, ere fate or mankind extirpated them.

The fishermen of Marloes were wont, in the past

summers of the nineteenth century, to fish for shellfish about the fertile shores of this islet. Now, so they will tell you, the weather is never continuously fine enough for them to risk such a venture. They have left the islet to the birds, and the gannets have profited thereby, increasing year by year in number.

Many are the tales the Marloes men can relate to you, if you lend a sympathetic ear, but you must wait on the greybeards, who alone can speak from experience of their own and of their forebears. There are tales of boats lost at moorings there in times of sudden groundswells, of marooned men, and of thrilling rescues; but there is no story of gentle times, and faithful winds. All these are forgotten in the memories of hard times, rough living and stormy days there, and of too fair breezes that drove the fishermen under reefed sail headlong to refuge in Dale, or Martinshaven. So this is the first tale of the sea's good nature and the wind's fairness to the first honeymoon on Grassholm. I should say, the first human honeymoon, remembering the gannets which enact their ridiculous love antics there in the spring.

These birds flew in hundreds above and about us as we sailed in towards the green shores of Graes-holm, to give it an ancient Scandinavian title, meaning the 'Green Islet.' We were approaching the east side, which is pleasantly green with long grass; the west side is snowy white with thousands of gannets. There are no havens, harbours, or beaches at Grassholm, only two or three narrow gashes in the rocks wide enough to allow of a boat entering and being moored safely, always provided there is no groundswell whatever. The smallest groundsea, as I found on another occasion, will roll in from the open sea and in less than a few minutes is capable of smashing any boat moored between the narrow rock walls.

On this occasion the gods were kind to us and gave us fair weather, so that we were able to moor the *Storm-Petrel* in the calm water of the southernmost gut in the low cliffs. Then we scrambled ashore with the same sort of feeling Columbus must have had when he scrambled (I am sure he did not walk as sedately as he is usually pictured as doing) ashore upon a western coast.

You might have thought that we should have at once rushed around the island sightseeing, eager, especially to examine the gannet colony, which, although out of sight of this quiet little landing-place in the rocks, assailed our ears with its uproar; a sound marvellously akin to the combined whirr of a dozen haycutting machines. The stench attacked our nostrils, and all the while a faint airy shower of the moulted white down from the young birds came eddying and dancing about us, borne by the north wind from the far end of this remote bird sanctuary.

No, we were wiser from much experience that told us hunger is no companion in the tranquil enjoyment of undiscovered lands. The two hours' sail in the boat and the task of mooring her off added to the keenness of the north wind and our natural appetites, had made us really hungry. So we sat down in the warm sunshine, under the lee of the cliffs, and ate and drank heartily.

'How long do we stay here?'

'That depends on the weather, and on how long you want to stay.'

'I was thinking of our water supply. At the rate we are drinking we shall be waterless by tonight.'

'There's supposed to be water here somewhere. We'll have a grand search presently. Meanwhile, I'm consumed with thirst—it must be excitement and salt air—I hope you are thirsty too, because you must drink cup for cup with me. All marooned adventurers do.'

When we were replete we packed up our stores and put them out of the hot sunshine behind a cool rock. From where we sat basking under the low cliff we could watch a group of seals also basking on some seaweed-covered rocks at the edge of the tide below us. The seals were singing a dirge among themselves, and every now and then the biggest of them, lying on the top of the rock, would raise his head (and his tail as well, to balance his head as he lay on his side) to utter a louder, musical moan that would start the others into renewed lamentations. The burden of their song is apparently heavy with lament; a dirge of the sea, yet pleasantly musical to the ordinary ear.

CHAPTER XVI

The Amenities of Grassholm

To describe the wonder of the gannet colony requires a powerful pen and a command of many choice superlatives. The whole upper cliff of the island's north-west corner, wherever there is foothold for a nest, is covered with the homes of these birds. As it was mid-July, the nests were occupied by young birds, mostly in the pure white downiness of extreme youth. A few nests contained a solitary egg, whilst a few had advanced in the other direction, and contained young already moulting their down for the first black plumage of adolescence. The gannet lays but one egg, rears but one young in the year, and the young gannet does not mature until its fourth or fifth year.

We realised later it was a mistake to walk about among nesting gannets. The nests, so many hummocks of flattened seaweed and grass, overlaid with trampled guano, were crowded together and on each hummock or pedestal sat a young bird with one parent brooding over it. Overhead flew thousands of other adults, their great white bodies filling the air like giant snowflakes. The adults deserted their babes as we came within touching distance, floundering away headlong from us in a confused mass, and beating their wings in an endeavour to rise up into the overcrowded air. Their long wings, threshing over the ground, often dealt the patient nestlings many a staggering blow.

On being displaced thus from their pedestals the young ones would hasten to get back, using their beaks to haul themselves up again, by digging them into the sides or tops of the nests. They quarrelled fiercely with each other when they happened to meet, and there was a rare set-to if one happened to mount on to the pedestal of another. They used their beaks freely until one or the other had been thrown overboard, king-of-the-castle fashion.

Their method of defence against human beings appeared to take the form of disgorging their last meal in front of us, and in pecking at approaching arms and legs. Often they would throw up a whole freshly swallowed herring, mackerel or pollack, and as we passed through the colony a trail of almost every kind of local fish was left in our wake by indignant nestlings, as well as by some of the adults.

The vastness of this colony can be pictured when it can be reckoned that there were three nests to one square yard, and that the colony covered a couple of acres of sloping cliff.

The uproar was now deafening and the stench, made up of the odours of dead fish, rotten seaweed, manure, and occasional dead birds—the whole encouraged by a warm sun—was well-nigh unendurable.

We left the colony and continued our exploration round the island, leisurely pointing out the beauties to each other, but carefully looking for a spring or well to renew our water supply.

The eastern side of Grassholm was pleasantly quiet after the turmoil of the gannetry. One may rest here, in soft long green grass, and listen to the gentle tinkle of the rock-pipits and the murmur of the swift tide as it runs past over the shallow ground and rocks half-awash below you. Here, safe from the more cruel storms from south and west, you may build your hermit's hut and live in a pleasant solitude. For company you will have the birds, the seals, a few flowers, and there is room for a large garden in the deep, peaty soil.

Such was my idle reverie as we basked in the sunshine on the soft couch of grass of that quiet eastern side, looking out toward the far mainland, Skomer and our own island.

Grassholm cannot be more than a score of acres in area all told, and is probably less, but it is so uneven that one cannot fairly estimate the acreage. The sea-birds crowd its western cliffs chiefly, and besides the gannets there are hundreds of guillemots, razorbills and kittiwakes. There are only one or two puffins and a few black-backed gulls. These, with one pair of oyster-catchers, a shag and some rock-pipits, were all the birds we saw. Seals are very numerous, and will entertain you with their songs and their disportiveness, if you can steal upon them unawares in the creeks. To count twenty seals lying along the edge of the rocks by the tide was a common occurrence.

We found water eventually, a mere drip tip-tapping from under a ledge of rock, and when we had gathered a tinful we found that even this was brackish. Still it was guaranteed to cure the thirsty and to take away all desire to drink from the merely moderately thirsty. Perhaps it would be quite palatable when boiled and cooled again. As it was it savoured of much salt and alas, of gannets, though this last flavour may have been owing to the ever-present effluvium of the gannetry which refused to leave us entirely in any part of the island.

From the highest point we watched the rich colours of the sunset foretell for us continuance of the gods' favours. The thousand flying bodies of the gannets took on a rosy hue as they flew over the coloured sea. Effortless on the gentle breeze, the long, black-tipped wings of the birds sustained their white bodies without quivering; only the long, pointed white tail moved as it steered the course, now up, now down, and now to one side. Groups of gannets flew out to sea upon fresh fishing adventures, and long lines and parties of returning birds came in with their harvest, already swallowed; for the young gannet helps himself from the parental gullet by inserting his beak therein, and is not fed with unsoiled fish straight from the sea as are most sea-birds.

Below us, below the seething gannetry, the tide was roaring from east and west northwards, for the northern stream strikes upon the south point of Grassholm and divides into two streams, which run along the east and west coasts to unite again at some point north of the island. One might well imagine Grassholm as a pebble dropped in midstream of some great river and lying half awash while the current streams furiously on each side of it; such is the strength of the spring tides there.

The colours lingered about the northern horizon during the starry night, and the full moon bathed us in light as we slept in the warm grass on the eastern slopes. Very little did we sleep, for youth and life were both combined with magic circumstance in keeping us wide awake to the beauty of the July moon, the sounds of the hurrying tide, the eerie cry of bird and moan of seal. Ever and anon I roused myself to listen more acutely to the tune of the sea, and to test the direction of the wind; but all night long the north wind soughed and sighed, saying, 'It is well, I blow softly; no other wind dares me. Sleep thou, thy boat is safe, the moorings are listless in the calm water.' For all I cared about was that the wind would stay immovable in the north all night, and thus keep our boat safe; for if the wind backed, who knew what swell or storm might rise in the night from south'ard?

Among other considerations, the lack of water was the chief reason for abandoning Grassholm on the following day. It was, therefore, agreed that we set sail for Ramsey Island at high water, while the northern stream had yet three hours to run, and so to help us northward to that lofty island. So we bade adieu to Grassholm and her gannets without sorrow, and with added eagerness to explore the new Lands of Ramsey, the Bishops and the Clerks.

CHAPTER XVII

We Visit the Bishops

In exactly three hours of nice sailing we arrived at Ramsey south harbour, and spent two days in this pleasant land, thanks to the hospitality of the resident farmer. In return, as he was interested in birds, we advised him that the 'big buzzard' he spoke of as haunting the island hills was really a golden eagle; the only one wild in all England and Wales. There was no mistaking the great bird's sweeping pinions, its size, and its shrill bark. I knew also that a pair of eagles had been set free many years ago on Skomer, and that this was, doubtless, the survivor. Ramsey has many rare and interesting birds and flowers, while her west coast is haunted by many seals.

But the time when we could thus idly cruise about from place to place was drawing to a close, for a return to work on our own island was becoming necessary. Therefore, bidding our host and hostess good-bye, we launched our boat and set out.

Even after so short a parting from the *Storm-Petrel* as two days made, it was good to be once more upon a tide, and liable to further wandering and adventure. The thought of the long cruise home filled us with pleasure. After all, an island-home is a perennial delight to return to after the smallest absence. The wind was still in the north: a fresh morning breeze which would die away and dwindle around the northern compass with the sun. We had promised ourselves a visit to all the Bishops and Clerks, those tide-harried rocks out to sea west of Ramsey, and that is why we first pointed north up Ramsey Sound, taking the last of the northern stream to carry us to the North Bishop.

The wind being east of north, and as soon as we had passed out of the northern mouth of the Sound, we turned north-west for our first destination and hoisted all our canvas to help.

The tides run very strongly about the maze of Bishops and Clerks rocks, and when we came up under the lee of the tall North Bishop the current was just beginning to run south. So we ran into a tiny creek in the cliff out of the way of the stream, and tied the *Storm-Petrel* to the rocks, letting her gently rub her fenders against the cliff as the slight backwash from the tide rocked her.

Thus, we claim to be of the enterprising few who have landed on this lonely rock, and, in accordance with the tradition which rules there, we added each our stone to the small cairn which marks the summit.

When you see a pile of stones on an eminence in deserted lands you may know the traditional ceremony at a glance. But we also removed a stone and carried it away with us for the very good reason that we required an anchor; having realized that it is better to anchor off in these places than to moor alongside, no matter how calm the anchorage or moorings. It saves paint, if not the more serious wear and tear to the wood.

The North Bishop comprises a chain of rocks in a straight line from sou'west to nor'east. The links are separated at high water by the tide, which rushes through with great force. I suppose, really, that the one high rock is really the Bishop, and the rest of them are his satellites or Clerks, attending him all in a row. One or two Clerks have strolled away on errands and got caught in the tide halfway to St David's or to Ramsey, or have wandered away towards the other Bishops, whom they may possibly serve. You may imagine one Bishop sending a messenger to another, for altogether there are four lofty, green-pated Bishops; first, my lord the North (or should he be the Archbishop?) then the Middle Bishop, the Little Bishop and finally the South Bishop.

Undoubtedly the finest fellow, and most closely followed by his retinue of Clerks, is the North Bishop, whom we had the honour to visit. Here resort many seafowl to rear their young, particularly guillemots, razor-bills and black-backed gulls. Seals attend, as everywhere here, and mallows grow in the sheltered niches of the rocks. The grass is long, wiry and slippery to the feet, and the whole place is much like a miniature Grassholm save in shape. There are, of course, no gannets, and the shape of this Bishop is thin and narrow—an ascetic fellow.

The Middle Bishop, to which we next set sail, is small, plump and well attended with acolytes and

Clerks. As far as we could see he is much like his Northern brother in having the same flora and fauna, and the same cruel tides. As we struck upon the north side, down which the current was pouring in a south-west direction, we had difficulty in finding a tideless anchorage. The *Storm-Petrel* could not stem the tide to work around to the south side and so seek a harbour there. We put in to one creek we found, but even here the tide was sneaking quietly through a crevice to the other side, and kept dragging us into the crack as soon as we shut off power.

Now I wished to land Doris at all the Bishops, but particularly at the South Bishop; for she has not seen, as I have, over the lighthouse there.

'You see here,' I explained in my best guide-book manner, pointing to the green head of the Middle Bishop looming above us as we lay under his bird-strewn cliff, 'a similar construction to the North Bishop, and occupied by seafowl of a similar kind. In fact, it is entirely similar, if smaller and less well known. Obviously, no one except shipwrecked people have ever landed here, for there is no cairn or sign of human hand. I propose we go ahead with the tide and visit the other two Bishops if we can, ere taking the last of the tide home. We'll try for the Little Bishop first.'

So we set out again, drifting into the roaring tide off this Middle Bishop. Unhappy mariners, untimely driven in rough weather, masters of ketches and schooners, know well the wicked ferocity of the currents that sweep south from the Bishops over foul ground.

We experienced these for the first time that day in our little ship, and though the day was calm, and a gentle zephyr smoothing along with the tide, the current nevertheless lifted, heaved, dipped and boiled as if a gale were a-blowing. Through this the *Storm-Petrel* bumped her way. The stream ran straight for the South Bishop, and had we wished to visit the Little Bishop we could scarcely have done so save by first preparing a plan to creep along the Middle Bishop shore, make a sharp tack to eastward, and fall back upon Little Bishop with the tide. As it was, we were unprepared, and finding ourselves in so good and true a course for the lighthouse, we gave the Little Bishop the cold shoulder. Poor forlorn fellow, there he lies, an out-at-heel dwarf, scarcely a Clerk to attend him, lonely like his greater neighbour, the South Bishop.

With all her canvas set and with a favouring breeze on her starboard from the north, with engine and with tide the good ship fairly raced towards the rock on which the lighthouse is perched. We got free from the worst of the heave when half a mile away from the Middle Bishop, and the *Storm-Petrel* settled down to sail in a steady, yacht-like manner.

As we drew nearer and nearer we could make out the steps of the lighthouse landing, and could see the three figures of the lighthousemen watching and waiting for us. It was quite a proud moment for us, for was not the *Storm-Petrel* racing in all her loveliness before critical eyes? Also, we were bringing news (we had remembered to commandeer a newspaper for them from Ramsey house), and it was also an opportunity for them to post letters. Therefore they were welcoming us fervently, if for selfish reasons.

The tide does not forget the South Bishop. It was nearly low water, and the current at its strongest of spring tide, but with the speed she had upon her the boat could defeat the stream. I hauled in the jib, then the lug, and unstepped the mast while Doris steered us through the tide into the small haven beside the steps.

All the conveniences for mooring a small boat obtain at the South Bishop, and in a few minutes we were climbing a rope-ladder ashore, after the *Storm-Petrel* had been moored off by an overhead cable stretched from cliff to cliff across the tiny haven. The lighthouse is perched on the summit of this tall and substantial rock, and an ascent is made by flights of steps cut out of the solid cliff.

There was something weighing upon the light-keepers' minds. This was clear as soon as we had introduced ourselves. The young supernumerary officer, whom I had met on my own island, introduced us to the chief and second officers, in all seriousness, 'Mr and Mrs Lockley . . . on their honeymoon!' Which, after all, was true, though we all laughed at his affected seriousness of mien. The ground thus broken, the supernumerary produced from his breast-pocket, as we were only halfway up the steps to the lighthouse, a treasured letter, and in a deprecatory, apologetic manner, said—

'Would you . . . could you . . . do you mind posting this letter for me when you get back ashore, please?'

As by magic, these words by the supernumerary caused the right hands of the chief and second officers to visit their own breast-pockets and to produce each a letter, all sealed and stamped ready.

'And if you please, this little letter, when you can find time to post it?'

'Do you mind . . . just this one as well?'

This was what had been troubling them probably ever since their keen eyes had seen our sail leaving Ramsey Sound early in the morning: the great problem of getting a letter to loved ones ashore; and this now in a fair way to be accomplished their minds were carefree again, and they ready to extend to us the utmost hospitality.

We were piloted over the spotlessly clean and shining rooms of the lighthouse, from the dazzling lantern-room to the shed where are housed the fog-signal engines. Everything was in perfect order, and it was clear that life here is one monotonous round of routine and watch, varied by spells of fog and mist, when extra work and appalling noise is occasioned by the engines driving compressed air for the booming siren. The sea might be calm or rough, the wind soft or loud, but routine goes on and on, as regular and as constant as the interminable smell of paraffin that clings to all lighthouses.

Of course there are days when the Relief is due, and a month ashore hoped for, weather permitting the boat to come. If you are something of a bird-lover, you can study the hundreds of birds dazzled by the powerful white light, that call there to rest upon the bird-ladders which have been provided by a very humane Royal Society for the Protection of Birds. But it was not now the migration season, and the place was deserted save for a stray pigeon and a few rock-pipits. Mallows grow here in the scanty grass, but there is little soil for gardening. We were further told that nothing would grow in any case owing to the millions of rock-lice that swarm everywhere after dark.

In the warm kitchen we were entertained to tea. The ancient visitors' book we signed had its first entry dated 1854. In return for their hospitality we left them some fresh milk and fruit, and the newspaper.

As we were about to step aboard our ship, homeward bound, the second officer tentatively remarked, 'If you should possibly be this way again, you will remember us and call for . . . letters?'

The others silently concurred with this reminder. So we cast off, drifted into the angry tide-race beyond the Rock, and into a wind which was now dead fair, sailing onward across the smooth sea for home in the late afternoon sunshine. Running before the breeze the sun was very warm upon our uncovered heads, and the tide served well. What hurry was there to reach home? I headed her for the mainland lodge, eleven miles across the bay, stopped the noisy infant, and let the *Storm-Petrel* go her quiet way. The stem parted the water with a gentle lapping which made us drowsy, so turn and turn about, we slept and steered, lying blissfully in the warm stern sheets.

These voyages were the first of many such in this and in succeeding summers.

CHAPTER XVIII

We Entertain

Our island was never so overcrowded with human beings as when, on a day in August, a cricket match was played in the north meadow. It came about through the issue of a challenge by mainland friends, to some of whom we owed much for hospitality and willing help in the past. It was our opportunity to repay some of this hospitality by inviting them to play the match on the island, and they accepted gladly. Though the thought of the sea journey caused the ladies of the party to shake their heads, they were very eager to have had the experience, and to see what manner of place it was that Doris and I were content to dwell in.

On our part we were not sure of raising a full team, but in the end, with the assistance of visitors, the three lightkeepers and John, we raised the required eleven. A calm day was essential to the success of the party, and in any case the mainlanders would not brave a breeze on the water. Therefore, when the first day of flat calm arrived we sailed over at sunrise, John and I, to fetch the opposing team.

At 9.30 a.m. Martinshaven beach was the scene of considerable excitement, as both *Storm-Petrel* and *Fox-*

trot were loaded with a burden of ten men and four ladies (comprising the eleven members of the opposing team, John, a visitor to the island, and myself). The ladies, all four very young, with sunburn and roses on their cheeks, occupied the place of honour in the *Storm-Petrel*. John was in charge of the *Foxtrot*, with its cargo of young men, and the cricketing outfit.

The *Storm-Petrel* took the *Foxtrot* in tow at the end of a length of rope. Jack Sound, almost rippleless at the slack of tide, caused wonder in the minds of those who thought only of its reputation for wrecks and rough seas. Halfway across the Broad Sound a little breeze sprang up, and John instantly hoisted sail so that the *Foxtrot* began to run down upon the *Storm-Petrel*. To remedy this I was fain to hoist sail too, and in this manner the two boats entered South Haven under full sail yet connected by the tow-rope. A few yards behind us swam a seal, prompted no doubt by curiosity.

South Haven was gaily decorated with every flag and piece of bunting the busy island team had been able to lay hands on. At the top of the landing-steps Edward, the donkey, was ready harnessed to the trucks, both donkey and trucks dressed in lofty plumes of bracken. The first item in the day's programme was a march to inspect the lighthouse. Edward was there to draw the ladies in the decorated trucks along the tram-line which runs from landing to lighthouse, a mile-long, up-hill journey.

The lighthouse aroused much admiration in those who had never seen over one. One comment of 'Why, I thought there was only a hut with a bit of wick in it!'

was surprising, coming as it did from folk who live on a coast bristling with lighthouses.

The journey back to the farmhouse, when the trucks loaded with the whole party were let go at full speed down the incline (Edward remaining behind, his services dispensed with) was fraught with screams and laughter. The last mad rush downhill was braked to a standstill by a careful lightkeeper, and the party found themselves in the home meadow. The island flag waved gently from the flagstaff on the hill above the house; and on the grassy lawn below, under streams of bunting, lunch was waiting the hungry folk. Exactly twenty-two people sat down to eat, this being probably the largest population ever assembled for such a purpose at the old house.

The island team were anxious to get a practice in before the match started. No one knew where our bowling or batting talent lay, while all modestly protested their incompetence. In the end we put up a good fight against the Marloes folk. Marloes were represented by four ladies, five men and two boys, we by five ladies and six men, but while Marloes had been practising for the event, we had had no opportunity.

On a high plateau of closely grazed meadow stumps were pitched. This ground had an additional advantage in that spectators and fielders commanded a wide and interesting view of the Broad Sound and the mainland, and all the traffic on the sea about the island, from Grassholm in the west to Linney Head in the south-east. Some trawlers that passed gave a friendly hoot on seeing so many white-clad figures on a lonely island. The incident that caused us the most amusement, however, was the running-aground of a ketch that came in too close to the shore. The helmsman, evidently anxious to see what was afoot on the island, sailed in close to the Stack, and with his eyes too much on the cricket-match, ran dead on to the seaweed-covered Tidball Rock near the Stack. As it was but an hour before low water of spring tide, there the ketch had to remain for two hours until the tide floated her off. On first striking we saw them hasten to lower the ship's boat and try to tow the vessel off. Quite in vain, however. Luckily the rock was soft with the summer growth of weed and the sea smooth. So all the crew could do for two hours was to watch the match!

The islanders batted first and were all out for 46. Then the mainlanders went in. We disposed of seven wickets for twenty runs, but their first man was still at the wicket, and he proved to be our greatest difficulty and finally our undoing. At last, with the score at forty-one he was caught out, and the remaining batters only raised the score to fifty-three. The Lower Island lost by 7 runs.

Before tea there was a bathing regatta in South Haven, where the two boats were moored side by side. After tea, on the grass as before, there were competitive games, and stunts with poles and pennies. Finally, before leaving the island, the mainlanders must needs see the creek where the *Alice Williams* had been wrecked, and inspect the store of coal and timber she had given us. Alice herself, newly painted, they had already seen on first entering South Haven, where she forever occupies a proud position on a rock overlooking the sea, her wooden body firmly bolted in that leaning position she so loved to affect in her seafaring days.

Towards sunset a move was made to the boats. Some young voices demanded to be allowed to stay the night in order to hear the 'cuckles and cock-lollies', as the shearwaters are locally termed. They were overruled, and presently both boats were sailing back for the mainland before a faint westerly breeze. Some last red flares were fired from boat and from island, as good-bye signals, ere the boats turned the corner out of sight of the islanders, who were waving and cheering so frantically on the landing-steps.

CHAPTER XIX

Wreck

Towards dusk only an ordinary gale was blowing. The sun had set behind racing clouds when I went out along the headland to bid good-night to my island. I wondered how soon the sea would go down to the measure of stillness required for a crossing to my home. Far out to sea in the south-west the red light of the island lighthouse winked me a reply. Westwards across Jack Sound lay the little island of Midland and beyond it the dark mass of Skomer and her gigantic Mewstone Rock.

Then quite suddenly I saw the bow and foremast of a ship silhouetted as it protruded from the black background of Midland. Sharply and clearly her bow stood out, her very keel showing beneath her forefoot. Then a monstrous billow rolled in and overwhelmed her. The end of things, I thought, filled with horror. But no! The great wave subsided, ebbed until the ship stood gaunt and naked as before, then, gathering strength, heaved up and buried her again. At the height of the gale, which had raged all day, she had been thrown on the rocks. Now the sea pounded her, and played with her as a cat with a mouse, before swallowing her completely. There was no light shining as a sign of life aboard, and no sound could reach across Jack Sound. The wind in my ears was such that I could barely hear the thunder of the surf two hundred feet below me.

I did not know then that thirty people were huddled amidships in a tiny cabin, shuddering at each of the ocean's blows. Nothing could live, surely, in that devastating sea!

Hardly had I left the headland than in the lane by my hut I met the first coastguard (arrived by car from the wireless station at Fishguard), who reported that the SS *Molesey* had wirelessed 'gone ashore on Wooltack Point.' That was the last message sent by her.

'A total loss; she'll never live in this sea!' he said.

He took down my depositions as to the position of the wreck on the south-east shore of Midland. She was certainly not on Wooltack Point, the headland on which we were standing, but immediately opposite us and quite out of reach half-a-mile across Jack Sound. No doubt her captain had confused the headlands in sending his message.

Hurrying back into the lane on our way to the village we met the male population coming solidly towards us in the dark, seated on or running behind a lorry loaded with the breeches buoy and life-saving rocket apparatus from St Ann's Head. Of no avail: no rocket could span Jack Sound; and as soon as the hopeless position of the wreck was known the lorry was turned back. Already the two local motor-life-boats, keen rivals, had, according to report, left their stations at Angle and St Davids, and were out searching.

The Marloes men must also help. As the only man to have seen the wreck properly, it was for me to organize a crew. Twenty men answered my appeal as one man. I called out the first five who showed their hands.

Nothing could be done that night in the howling wind. The rendezvous was Martinshaven at dawn, where we would launch our biggest boat. But long before dawn we were out upon the headland, sleep far from us, our hearts longing for the wind to abate. We watched the white run of the tide anxiously.

It must have been at low water that at last a sign of life came from the darkness where I knew the ship was lying. One or two rockets shot up, their blue light revealing an iron deck swept as bare as the palm of my hand. Encouraged by this unexpected glimpse, with new hope in our hearts, we ran down to the dark cove where the boats lay. Just as our scratch crew was launching, the headlights of a car drew down upon the beach. The principals of the firm owning the *Molesey* hastened to tell us that there were some thirty souls comprising the crew of the wrecked ship.

The sky in the east was growing pale when we set out, unwillingly pushing back half-a-dozen volunteers who would have overloaded us. The six of us rowed and rowed, for my part as never before, with those long sea-sweeps. Half-a-mile of such pulling brought us to that rocky cauldron of wind-roughened currents which is Jack Sound.

It was now light enough for us to see the *Molesey* lying tilted against Midland, her smokestack flat as cardboard, her bridge and upperworks carried right away. There was life on board, however, and we pulled harder than ever, gaining slowly foot by foot with tide and oars against the fierce west wind.

We were less than one hundred yards from the wreck, toiling painfully but surely along, tossed and battered by the swell, when the Angle lifeboat, new, full-powered with twin engines, came grandly up from southwards at top speed, crashing through the waves as she swept in front of us. Throwing out anchors, she paid them out until she had drawn alongside the wreck. One by one the survivors threw themselves down upon her. There were more than eight missing, reported swept overboard in the night.

Pleased that these were saved, yet, I must confess, disappointed to have had no share in their rescue, we drifted back upon the island of Midland. With some difficulty we put ashore a landing-party to see if any survivors had reached the island in the night. There were none. A few minutes later the wind had blown us back to Martinshaven.*

I was anxious now to return to my island, but it was much too rough to cross that day. Even on the following morning it was none too pleasant when John and I set out. Our course lay past the *Molesey*. We were tempted to board her and explore. Something of John's fever to loot and pillage a wreck had by now crept into my veins. We reduced speed as we passed her. All doubts as to whether we had better

* It must be said that subsequently the owners of the *Molesey* recognized the Marloes crew's efforts by presenting them with a handsome cheque.

stop, in view of the sightseers, now rapidly crowding on to the headland opposite, were dispelled when we heard a feeble call from near the ship.

One last survivor, a Maltese fireman, yesterday hidden, semi-conscious, in a berth during the lifeboat rescue, and now supposing all others drowned but himself, was signalling desperately to us. He had jumped into the sea with nothing but a lifebelt and vest on, and was now standing on the rocks below the ship. Almost before we were alongside he fell into the *Storm-Petrel*, over-eagerly, bruising his already battered body, half-frozen, trembling with fright and exposure.

We could get no sense out of him, so I left him with John, and while he was being fed out of our stores, wrapped warmly and given the thing he craved most—tobacco—I scrambled aboard the wreck to look for other survivors. In vain; I saw only things which saddened me—or aroused cupidity.

We sped back with Pola Attard to Martinshaven, left him in good hands there, and then sailed home once more, to hear Doris's thrilling account of the wreck and the rescue, as seen from our island.

We never got a chance, unfortunately, to raid the *Molesey*, as we did to our hearts' content the *Alice Williams*. Afterwards we learned that no one was allowed to remove or salvage a single item during the two calm days that followed. All her beautiful furniture, her tools and fittings were senselessly sacrificed by the underwriters to the gale that soon came and swept her to the bottom. Her furniture and wooden parts, battered to uselessness, floated away to distant beaches, and were picked up for firewood. I regretted especially a nice lathe I saw on her.

Now only the iron heart of her lies visible at dead low water of spring tides, given over to the fishes and the long ribbony seaweeds.

CHAPTER XX

The Story of the Shearwater

So little reliable information on the habits of the Manx shearwater could we find in our bird-books that we determined to discover the birds' life-story for ourselves, in as far as the periods of incubation and fledging-time were concerned.

We knew already that the shearwater arrived very early in the year on the island. In an observation of three years we found that it arrived regularly some time early in February, but it was not until mid-March that these birds began to call each night in any number. From that time onwards until the middle of August they screamed each night over the house, as they passed to and from their nests in the rabbit-holes. Their strange note I have already described.

Late during the day the shearwaters begin to come in towards the island from the far open sea. One by one they collect until sometimes there are thousands in a flock. They sweep up towards the island from the Bristol Channel. If the weather is misty they arrive in the vicinity of the two islands, Skomer and this island, where they breed, some hours before dark, but in clear weather they may not appear until dusk. Other birds, perhaps from St George's Channel and northwards, converge upon the islands from the west, and still others sweep down St Bride's Bay from the north.

However numerous they may be on the sea near the island they do not land until two hours after sunset, and they may be later if there is a clear sky, or if the moon is shining. The birds do not like the moon, and are much less noisy in moonlight. The darker and more stormy the night, with plenty of wind and rain, the more they revel in it, and the more they scream.

At the appointed time one may confidently expect to hear the scream of the first bird venturing inland, and in a few minutes there will be hundreds more screaming; then, if you go out-of-doors, you can hear the swish of their wings as they glide past you at a terrific speed.

It is strange that these swift-flying birds can suddenly check their flight and drop with perfect accuracy in the dark upon their chosen rabbit-hole, even where that hole is amongst the crowded entrances and exits of a rabbit-warren. It is, however, just as well that the bird can do this, for the shearwater is a very indifferent traveller on land, progressing by means of a series of short little runs on its toes. It cannot balance itself when stationary, but has to rest flat on its breast, its legs being placed rather far back on its body. On rough ground it scrambles along by using its half-outspread wings and pushing with its feet.

How do the shearwaters know each his own rabbit-hole? And how, in the first place, do they find one to suit them? I suppose the old birds know where to go from past experience, and apparently they have an exceptionally keen eyesight or instinct in the dark. I have seen a pair home-hunting in the spring, exploring the holes and crannies along the foot of a hedge. They find out the most isolated and hidden burrows as well as the crowded warrens. We found that each year the same pairs returned to the same holes, so that, in spite of all their wide wanderings over the Atlantic in mid-winter, they evidently pair for life.

The nest is made in the recess at the end of a burrow, no matter if the burrow is many yards long and far from the surface, or if it is only a blind shaft a few feet long. The shearwater collects whatever it can find in or near the burrow to make a lining for the nest, such as dried grass, dead bracken fragments, and rootlets torn from the walls of the burrow. Here it lays its solitary white egg some time in May, or late in April.

We found that before the egg was laid the parents were very irregular in their sojourns by day at the nest. Sometimes one bird would stay, sometimes the other, often both or neither. Each night they would meet together at the mouth of the burrow and indulge in amorous billing and cooing, this I mean very literally, for they would caress each other with their bills, and at the same time coo the most unearthly and laughable cooings it is possible to imagine.

However, when once the egg was laid they carried on their flirtations underground. Under no circumstances would the birds leave the egg alone, and exposed to the risks of unwelcome rabbits or other birds. In turns they incubated it, one bird staying at the nest for from two to five days at a stretch, and as far as we could discover, the sitting bird did not leave the nest at all on these occasions, nor was it ever fed by its mate visiting it during these spells of incubation. They were very tenacious and anxious about their one egg, and would peck our hands fiercely when we came once each day to examine the egg.

To enable us to make this study we had marked several nests, and cut a sod of earth out of the ground just above each nest, so that, at any time, by lifting up this sod, we could study the progress of the egg, and later of the chick.

We expected the egg to hatch at any time after four weeks had passed, but it was not until after the seventh week that signs of hatching were observed. In one case the chick had only just emerged on the 52nd day. In another nest we could hear the chick cheeping in the egg on the 52nd day, but this bird did not emerge until the 54th day.

The parents brooded the nestling in each case for one week, day and night, but afterwards they only came to feed it at night, when both parents would hold long conversations with the nestling in the recess. It was very amusing to hear the absurd cooing of the parents and the faint, occasional 'peep-peep-peep', very querulous and low, of the downy chick.

Of all the downy chicks of the bird world it would be difficult to find such a powder-puff as the baby shearwater at six weeks old. It grows two lots of down, the first remaining attached to the second, so that, at six weeks, it is an immense ball of slate-grey down from which only the long beak protrudes. The bright, beady, black eyes are almost hidden by the down of the head.

Shortly after sprouting its feathers the young bird is entirely deserted by its one-time loving parents. By placing a sod at the mouth of the burrow, by its position we were able to note whether a bird had entered or left the burrow, and thus to discover how long the nestling remained unfed in the nest. In each case it was about the sixtieth day that the young one, still very downy and not fully feathered, was completely deserted.

Six days after the young bird bestirred itself from the nest and made its first journey to the mouth of the burrow, pushing aside the sod, and leaving a trail of down at the burrow mouth to give evidence of its activity. It did not venture further than the mouth of the burrow, but stayed there almost immovable during the midnight hours, an almost tragic figure. We felt quite a compassion for the lonely little fellow, now seven days deserted and hungry. Wherever we walked on the island at night in early September these hungry lonely little figures could be seen sitting patiently at the mouths of the rabbit-burrows, waiting perhaps for the parents that would never come again. Before dawn they would return to their nests.

The next night and for six nights all told did our two specially marked birds keep vigil, and then after those twelve days of fast they at last made off to the sea, and we did not see them again.

This journey from the nest to the sea is one of the most perilous adventures of these youngsters' lives. They are lucky if they have a high wind blowing when they first make up their minds to start, for a strong wind will often enable them to fly all the way from nest to sea, by giving them the necessary 'lift' upwards when they beat their wings in trying to rise off the ground.

The newly fledged shearwater is very unsteady on its legs and cannot make short runs on its toes as the adults can. If there is no wind it patters along the ground somehow, sustaining itself by beating its wings in the air, a most exhausting process which compels it to rest often. On uneven ground it pushes along with wings and legs, using its beak as well to surmount high objects.

It is a strange sight to see, in the dusk of night, these young birds making impulsive flutterings and scramblings, and anon resting awhile, towards the sea. They have great need to reach the sea the same night upon which they start from their nest. Should they be unable to do this, but instead find themselves still on land when dawn comes, their chances of remaining alive until the next evening are rather slender.

Almost before it is light the black-backed gulls are beating over the fields and burrows and searching for these helpless young birds. The light of day seems to render the birds even more helpless and incapable of resistance. Besides the black-backed gulls, the herring gulls, the crows and the buzzards all eagerly kill and devour the stranded young shearwaters in a variety of cruel ways peculiar to each bird of prey. On calm nights even the adult shearwaters are sometimes unable to rise from heather and bracken, when they too are caught in the open upon the following day and killed. The toll is very heavy, and in one season I could reckon the remains of over fifteen hundred birds on the island cliffs and meadows.

The young birds tumble straight over the cliffs when they reach them, at night, and flutter down into the sea. Here, at last, they are in their own element, a limitless place where food and drink can be found. One bird we carried to the sea first alleviated its thirst by daintily drinking and then proceeded to wash itself very thoroughly. All the young birds are expert swimmers and divers, using their wings and feet to swim with under water. One imagines that they have little difficulty in quickly obtaining a meal of sprats or fry and thus breaking their long fast.

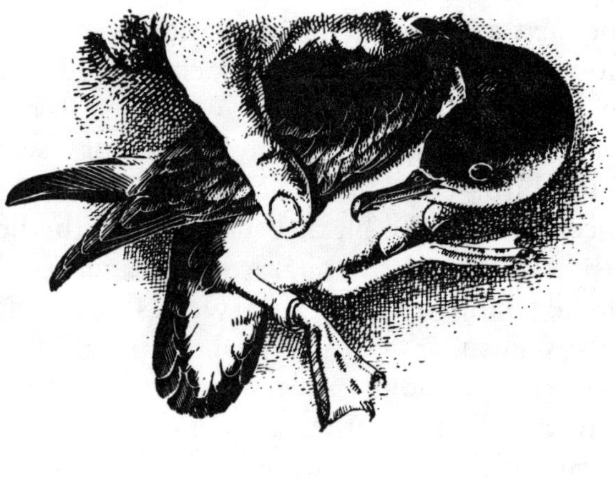

CHAPTER XXI

A Rabbit's Life

The rabbit-burrows here are the scene of great competition from February onwards. No sooner has the rabbit in February begun seriously to consider nesting operations than the shearwater arrives in the burrow. The island rabbit, which varies somewhat from the ordinary mainland rabbit in that it is smaller and has slightly darker and longer fur, does not begin to breed very early. Then, in April, the ubiquitous Mr Puffin arrives, demanding his share of the burrow.

It is a source of wonder to me where the doe rabbit actually hides her young. Most of the newly weaned young ones appear from holes which are definitely known to harbour shearwaters or puffins or both. Somewhere in the labyrinth below the doe must have found a corner in which to make her nest. First she tears mouthfuls of coarse grass and carries this below, next she lines the grassy nest with her own fur, torn from belly and breast so as to bare her teats for suckling. Here the naked, blind babies are hidden, the doe plucking more fur to cover them deeply. Finally she covers the nest with more grass, and often with earth, so heavily that one might expect the babies to be stifled. Once a day, or possibly twice, she opens the nest to feed them, covering them over again while they are still blind and helpless during the first nine days. After this period the young ones open their eyes and begin to scramble about, having already grown a thick brown baby coat, and a few days later they learn to run to the mouth of the burrow and nibble grass for the first time.

The doe forgets her first family when they are three weeks old and prepares a new nest for the second family. Her fecundity is amazing. After the first family in March, she has at least two and generally three more at monthly intervals, in April, May, June and even July. If she is a strong doe in her prime she may breed as many as five litters of four young ones in each, or twenty in the season. The March-born rabbits themselves breed before they are three months old, the does having one family in June and at least another a month later. The April-born may breed once in the same summer. The number of young in litters born to these young does is invariably very few, generally but two, occasionally three and rarely four. The old does will sometimes have six in one litter, often five, but usually four.

The mainland doe-rabbit often makes her nest in a specially-dug shaft a few feet long, the entrance to which she blocks with earth and turf. This for her is a wise precaution against marauding stoats and weasels, but is not necessary to the island doe, which follows this procedure but rarely. There are no stoats or weasels, in fact nothing more harmful than mice, frogs, newts, and slow-worms in the way of creeping animals, on the island.

From the birds, however, the rabbits have to suffer much. They are liable to have their noses or tails severely tweaked by the puffin's sharp beak, or to be held and wrenched by the shearwater's long, hooked bill, should they encounter either of the birds below ground, as they must frequently do.

The shearwaters in particular are the usurpers of the burrows the rabbits have dug for themselves, for they follow the windings of the warrens to their farthest depths. They occupy the burrows until every available recess is engaged by a pair. On more than one occasion two pairs of shearwaters have occupied the same recess until one has been able to assert its right by laying the egg before the other pair did; and even then we noted an instance where a third bird brooded for one day the egg belonging to another pair. We put numbered rings on the legs of several birds and were thus able to make this interesting discovery. On another occasion we found a shearwater brooding, or rather sitting, on top of a nest of blind young rabbits.

The puffin can drive away a rabbit by worrying it with its sharp beak, and almost all the short burrows and blind shafts within easy distance of the sea are occupied by Mr Puffin, to the exclusion of the rabbits and of most of the shearwaters. Many of the latter, however, occupy burrows opening upon or near, those of the puffin, and as a result the two species not infrequently come up against each other in a battle royal. I have heard them scrapping below ground, and twice have I seen them come rolling out of the burrow, locked in a flurry of wings and legs, and stabbing, wrenching beaks. Once out in the daylight the puffin flew away into the sunshine as befitted a bird active all day, whilst the shearwater, a night-lover, hastened back to the gloom of the burrow; incidentally carrying off the honours of war.

Altogether, the overcrowding below ground is amazing, and productive of endless curious accidents, both grave and gay. For instance, a puffin incubated a shearwater's egg for a few days on one occasion until the egg got broken. The puffin then deserted it, leaving the burrow and its broken egg to the unfortunate shearwater. I have also a record of a puffin routing out a nest of newly born rabbits from a short burrow. The poor babies were found crawling at the mouth of the burrow, and soon made a meal for a hungry gull.

All these three dwellers underground have a common enemy in the gulls. As I have recorded elsewhere, these marauders search all day for young rabbits, and are equally ready to pounce on an unsuspecting puffin emerging from its burrow. Of the three gulls the herring gull is the mildest offender. Most of these confine their activities to fishing at sea, but a few depraved individuals earn an easier living by preying upon the inmates of the burrows, and by robbing the guillemots and razorbills of their hard-sought-for fish and, where possible, of their eggs.

A fourth invader of the rabbit burrows is the storm-petrel, which arrives at the end of April. This little fellow, however, in no way incommodes the other burrow-dwellers, but rather keeps out of their way, using only the small holes and crevices at the mouth of the burrows in which to nest. Like the shearwater it spends well over a month incubating its solitary egg, which it lays late in May, or in June, and then more than two months in rearing the nestling, so that we sometimes find a late youngster still in the nest in November.

CHAPTER XXII

The Adventure of the Newly Discovered Passage

Summers have their endings, and winter perforce must come with all its wild storms and rough seas. We had many winter adventures; not all of them I should care to experience again, but this one was pleasant enough.

Doris, I and John had left the island on Friday with a gale from the sou'west threatening us, and the breeze that blew us across to the mainland was already so fresh that the infant motor was unnecessary and the lug had to be reefed.

The gale came on in the afternoon, and blew until Saturday at midnight, when it abated, so we prepared to return at dawn on Sunday morning. The breeze was now west and still so fresh that John, deeming it impossible for us to get down to the island, remained in the village, intending to come down to the Haven at the proper time of tide for the passage to the island.

The red sky of morning threatened a day of bad weather and, as the one responsible for the ferrying of the rabbit-catch from the island, I was anxious to go and bring it to the mainland, and then return to the island. In coarse weather it is not safe to travel up and down these Sounds with a crew of oneself and one's wife. Two men are needed, both able, if required, to pull a fourteen-foot oar for hours at a time. Though if one is sure of a fair breeze it is another matter.

Now Doris and I were, as soon as the wind began to fall to a gentle sailing breeze, seized with sea-fever again, and we put to sea alone, intending to cruise about St Bride's Bay until it was time to take the current for our island. I am not ashamed to say that I love our boat, and whenever there's a pleasant sailing breeze my desire is to be sailing her. I love best a beam wind, for then the boat sails with tight sheets, heels over a little and cuts bravely through the water. There was an extra exhilaration to-day because we had not been able to sail about alone for several days; moreover, the Skomer boat had just left the Haven to return to Skomer, and as we pushed our boat down the pebbles to launch her was even then creeping sluggishly towards Skomer, soullessly hugging the rocks so as to keep out of the wind. There were five people aboard this Skomer boat, and all five could appreciate the sight of a full-rigged boat beating against a headwind.

There was not enough wind to beat without the help of the 'Infant', so we started her bawling as soon as we pushed off, and I began, with sailorly pleasure, to hoist sail. First I stepped our tall white mast, then I ran up the white lug-mainsail. Doris headed her after the Skomer boat, which was nearly at Skomer by now, while I ran up the jib.

I must record that a bowsprit is a serious inconvenience when we are launching or landing our boat in the narrow gut of the boatslip on the island, and in consequence I make an oar serve as a bowsprit by tying it to one thwart and to the ring in the stem of the boat, so that some three feet of the handle-end protrudes from the bow in the true fashion of all self-respecting bowsprits. To the extreme end of the oar the jib is tied. On this occasion I ran up the jib, and made it all fast. The *Storm-Petrel* caught the west wind on her port beam, heeled over deliciously, and with the Infant helping shaped a course for Skomer North Haven, heading N.W. by W. on this first tack. I hope and believe the poor men of Skomer, rowing their tub-like craft like galley-slaves, saw the white sides of the *Storm-Petrel* as she lay over to the breeze, saw her red gunwale-line making a margin below her white mainsail, her flying, white jib out upon the bowsprit, and enjoyed the rare sight. Such is the conceit of boat-owners!

Incredible as it may seem (for such *voyageurs*) Doris had never been in the North Haven of Skomer, and it was our intention to tack leisurely into this little harbour upon the heels, so to speak, of the Skomer boat. Doris would then have had the opportunity of admiring that very lovely haven, and if our good friends the residents invited us ashore—well, all such little adventures are welcome. There is no greater freedom or adventure than that of sailing one's own boat to foreign shores.

When we had stood out long enough on this first tack, long enough for us to see that the Skomer boat had landed and was being hauled up the little beach there, we came about and headed S.W. on the second tack, making for the Rye rocks of North Haven. The Little Sound lay invitingly before us, with our own island far below. How easy it seemed to go on down to our home with this pleasant breeze to help defeat the tide that must perforce be all against us. The temptation was too much for us. The sky was half-filled with heavy rainclouds to the south; the north was full of blue, rapidly diminishing as the clouds came out of the west. The current was already making up through the Little Sound against us. Nevertheless, the *Storm-Petrel* urged us to be sailing across the open seas for home, and we abandoned ourselves to her mood, forgetting our cruise to Skomer North Haven; forgetting the astonished men of Skomer, whose traditions of tide we might be destroying; only glad to be sailing in full canvas for the shores of our distant island. The Infant cried joyously to be battling a tide again, and we let the boat point due south through the Little Sound, slackening the sheets to take a fairer wind. There was a short tussle with the tide where it ran strongest in the Little Sound, but the *Storm-Petrel* emerged triumphant and sailed away across the sea for our island.

The rest was easy. It suited the boat to be dragged out westward a little by the tide, as this enabled us to sail with a fairer breeze. We reached the Stack, the nearest point of the island, in thirty minutes and easily defeated the north-west-going current there. A few minutes later we were in our own harbour, restless South Haven, as pleased as two mortals could be, and a quarter of an hour later we had loaded our cargo and the Infant was taking us out of the harbour on our voyage back to the mainland.

The wind had now dwindled to the faintest breeze, which barely filled our mainsail, and out of which it was continuously being spilt by the lumpiness of the ground sea, which caused the boat to roll and bump. The clouds in the west had been quietly gathering and now a heavy squall of rain hung over us, threatening to deluge us at any moment. Though the sail hung almost idly, and I was helping the Infant with one oar, I had a not quite comfortable feeling that presently the mainsail would be more than enough to drive us to the Haven on the mainland. And so it proved.

A sailing breeze sprang up as the rain began to fall, and in a few moments it freshened as the rain became heavier. Before I could comfortably make up my mind to reef the mainsail (the jib, of course, was not out), rain and wind became violent and we were driven furiously into Jack Sound, the sea suddenly presenting a spectacle of wind-driven white horses. The Infant was of no use at all, and roared louder and louder as the wind carried the boat at a break-mast speed. A rabbit-catcher working on the cliffs above Jack Sound described to me later that our pace had been 'marvellous', a truly descriptive adjective, and one calculated to please a boat-lover. We turned the corner into the Haven eventually with no little relief, and the sail flapped under the shelter of the rocky shore. The Infant ceased its useless roar and settled down quietly to the business of bringing us to the Haven's pebble beach.

CHAPTER XXIII

We Add to Our Number

There are some people in the world who have no sense of fear; Doris is one of them. For my part I have to admit to little fears and flutterings at moments of necessary decision or crisis. Doris is perpetually prepared to go out to sea in the face of any reasonable gale, and it is hard for me to say her nay when she expects to put forth in a mild hurricane. It is, besides, damaging to one's self-esteem to have to admit that it cannot be done, no matter how prudent the decision may be. If we do not fare forth and the wind falls a little one is a little disgusted with oneself. If a gale really does blow all one feels is a little smug satisfaction, the merest ghost of a feeling.

It is hard, therefore, to decide what to do when the wind is only half a gale and half a breeze. Can one put to sea? Wisdom will whisper nay, youth and action dictate yea. Presently, I feel sure, experience will tell us how unwise it is to set out at all in bad weather. For the day on which the following adventure befell proved to be one of bad weather, indeed, and I have no wish to repeat the experience.

The blame, if any, must partly be laid upon Richard, my rabbit-catcher, of whom more anon.

One bright morning, in October, after a day or two of rough weather, Doris and I left the island in charge of John and Henry, as we often did, and sailed to Martinshaven. I say sailed, but it was only a pretence of sailing. What little breeze there was about was rendered useless by the groundswell, which upset it from out the sails. Still it is, next to actual sailing, a fine thing to pretend to sail—to have all the canvas out in full glory with sheets tight to prevent undue flapping. On this occasion the Infant was moving all the while along with the tide, and I helping with a lazy oar.

We got to the Haven, disgorged our cargo, and hauled the boat above the tide with the handwinch. Richard had promised to meet us, and come back to work on the island. But he failed to appear, and after waiting for several hours, during which we were busier about other things than merely waiting for a procrastinating rabbit-catcher, I went over on my bicycle to hunt him down in his native village.

Tracking a man of moods, such as Richard is, is no easy task, and on this occasion it meant the visiting of several cottages, where I was given all the local gossip as to Richard's past, present and future movements. It chiefly appeared that Richard had been playing an auctioneering game with the lords of the islands, with Me (of the Lower Island), and with Him of Skomer, to wit. He had been trying to sell himself for a higher wage to Skomer, well knowing that I was not willing to pay more than his usual wage, which, as a matter of fact, is above the standard rate.

Richard is an old man, yet clever at his profession, and one has perforce to take his peculiarities as they come. I could write many pages about him, but not now, for I have not yet come to the Adventure of which I would speak. Let me finish with Richard for the present by adding that I found him in his cottage garden, and being already armed with the knowledge that he would get no more wages on Skomer, I threatened him with a mild ultimatum that his last chance this winter would be tomorrow, when he must finally decide to be, or not to be, ready on the beach at sunrise. For it was now dusk and too late to think of crossing that night. Richard promised, faithfully, again, to turn up in the morning.

The sunrise next day was lurid and stormy, and with a faint heart I looked out upon the sea, which was running high by reason of a strong west wind. It was not fit weather to cross. Richard would not face it, I knew, and he did not even put in an appearance. To consult Doris under the circumstances seemed the only thing to do, so I laid the case before her.

'We can get down to the Lower Island if we go at once, and provided the Infant keeps her song true and steady. Also, I think there's a possibility of sailing if the wind goes up a little.' Doris was fearless in the matter, but experience had taught her by now to leave our fate in my hands for decision.

Now, as I say, it is difficult to say nay when your wife looks so ready and courageous enough to tackle anything with you. I had not therefore the heart to say nay while there was a fair chance. To-day I had only half a heart to go and half to stay. The casting vote was given by Doris, who merely said nothing and looked much. So we set forth.

Lustily roared the Infant, knowing what need we had of her, and I pulled a hearty oar, while Doris took the tiller. The sea was all of a smother at Tusker Rock, but we safely crossed Jack Sound and pointed her to windward. We could not make our 'westing' enough to put up sail, and I was sorry we had not gone through the Little Sound instead of Jack Sound. I soon saw, too, that we were going to have our work cut out to reach the Island at all, for the tide and wind were both going east. The Infant did its best; I did mine with an oar, and if looks could have helped Doris, who was thoroughly enjoying it, including the salt spray, would have got us home in good time. But without any warning to me, for I sat rowing back to the bow, a green sea came inboard, effectually silencing the Infant as it washed down past the engine into the bilge-trap. There was nothing now to be done save to bail this green fellow out as quickly as possible, and this I set out to do at once, while Doris kept the boat's head on to the seas with the paddles. The wind had been freshening all the time, and drove us eastwards while the tide dragged us south.

Bailing completed, I tried to persuade the wet and discomforted Infant to recommence work. She did her best but, after a few apologetic coughs, was unable to oblige us. Clearly she wanted a good cleaning and drying. Meanwhile our beloved Island home drifted to windward and we to leeward. We saw our harbour come into view, looking green and sweet, but far away to windward and unget-at-able. Once chance now was left to us: to put up sail and run for it before the wind to Milford Haven, braving the tumultuous seas and striving tide-races outside St Ann's head.

Fairly caught in the tide now, the *Storm-Petrel* tossed, dipped and curvetted as she was borne towards St Ann's by the wind-roughened tide. I reefed the lug mainsail, stepped our tall, white mast with a little effort owing to the tossing of the boat, and ran up the canvas. Instantly the boat gave up her sluggish drifting and leaped forward with delight. I made one last effort before I let her run away. The sheet was close-hauled, and the *Storm-Petrel* headed for the Island while I again tackled the engine. But all things were against us. The sheet flapped in the headwind and we began to go astern; the tide carried us away and the Infant failed to bawl. So we turned around and let her go for Milford Haven and the high, white-crested rollers that pounded on the cliffs of St Ann's head.

The *Storm-Petrel* is a noble vessel, and well built to stand work on the open sea. As she flew away before the gale, she rode the seas grandly, barely shipping as much as a gallon of water. Sometimes the big rollers curled over and crashed behind and before us, but she moved faster than these breakers and slipped away from beneath them. Now her bow would be six feet clear, standing in the air on the crest of a wave, and then she would plunge down the slope and her nose would be level with the water, which would look over the gunwale with intent to enter and swamp us; but our brave boat would rise eagerly, shaking the water from her dripping freeboard and resume the race again.

After a little while, and after some very formidable

breakers had been negotiated without serious distress to the boat, I began to take pleasure in the thrilling experience we were having. I was assured by her behaviour that the *Storm-Petrel* would weather all the seas in front as easily as she had done those behind. As for Doris, that fearless lady had enjoyed every anxious second, I do believe, and was completely happy when we both sat in the stern thwart and settled down together on this wild cruise for shelter.

We afterwards found that John and Henry had watched our whole performance from the island, and the men at the island lighthouse had been standing by to send up signals as soon as an extra big wave engulfed us. This was very courteous of the latter, though when we passed St Ann's Head the coastguards there did not appear to have seen us at all, even when we were in the midst of the tide-races of the south stream from the Channel, and the ebb tide of Milford Haven, which, at this point, and at certain hours of every day, strive together in motley confusion.

However, there was no need for undue anxiety. The *Storm-Petrel* passed through the inferno at St Ann's Head without taking any water inboard, and sailed on up Milford Haven to the quiet waters of the bays and inlets there. Dale Roads was full of ships taking shelter in that anchorage, and two trawlers, going out to sea from Milford Dock, turned back on encountering the swell from St Ann's and made for the same place. Even in these Roads the west wind made a choppy sea, and I preferred to sail on to Sandy Haven, where we could obtain perfect security, quietness and hospitality for the night.

The tide was at low water so we had to wait our chance to sail up the creek of Sandy Haven. We eventually ran ashore on some pebbles east of Great Castle Head, had a meal, basked for a little in the sun, and when the tide was nearing full flood continued up the creek. I had dealt firmly with the Infant meanwhile, and she sang bravely again, landing us in proper fashion beside Sandy Haven quay.

The owner of this quay is Captain Cristal, that very useful gentleman who assisted us to dismantle the *Alice Williams*. He extended a hearty welcome, and made us free of his house, while his amiable wife prepared us that warm meal which hungry *voyageurs* are so capable of appreciating.

There is a magic stillness in the air of Sandy Haven, and we slept soundly in that windless place where nothing can ever happen; where gales are not heard; where the water is perpetually smooth, and where a man may lay down to sleep without fear for his ship's safety.

We were duly acquainted with the history and local gossip of the neighbourhood from our good hostess, and learnt, among other things, that a kitten might be had for the asking at a place up the creek on the opposite shore. Our cruise was, therefore, not to be a fruitless run and only for shelter. From that moment it was apparent that our whole object had been to obtain a kitten from some place inside Milford Haven.

While the tide was still making that night we went across in the *Storm-Petrel* and were given a pretty white and tabby-marked kitten. He was promptly stowed on board, made cabin-boy and named 'Mousse'.

The next morning was cold and rainy, and with faint hope in our hearts we sailed away at dawn, going down to Dale on an easterly breeze. A mighty swell came rolling in from the Atlantic, and it was clearly blowing hard outside St Ann's. We therefore put about and motored back to Sandy Haven, running aground just before the tide ebbed too far to allow our getting up the creek. We then left the *Storm-Petrel* there on the mud and explored the by-lanes of this foreign country, the rain having now been blown away by a wind from E.N.E.

When the tide came in, late in the afternoon, we bade adieu to our host and hostess, with many thanks for harbourage of boat and man, and, not forgetting Mousse, set sail with better heart for the open sea. There was still a heavy swell, but the sea was unbroken and the breeze fair all the way home. The only difficulty now would be in landing in the surf of the swell. I prayed that my good John and Henry would be standing by at the winch to haul the boat up as soon as she touched our crazy slipway. Two coastguards looked at us curiously as we passed under the cliffs of St Ann's, the *Storm-Petrel* in full sail, mainsail and jib-upon-bowsprit, riding the angry swell with untroubled serenity. Tide and wind were in our favour, and we made a glorious passage over the sunset-coloured sea. The sun dropped behind the island as we approached, but we could see our little harbour white with the dancing temper of the ground-sea, a last legacy of the storm.

The only thing to do was to make a painter ready on her bow, run in upon the slip with the Infant's help, trust that the gods would restrain the wash of the sea for the space of time required to make the boat fast to the cable and so haul her clear of the angry swell. It was a ticklish business. Three hands held to the painter, and as the swells came rushing in and lifted the stern of the boat, all three hauled mightily; the fourth man lustily wound the slack wire tight on the winch, till presently the cable tautened and the good ship shook the water off her to ride gently up the rough slip and to come to rest in her steep berth.

What a delight there is in an island home when one lands and makes safe the boat after either a perilous or calm voyage: more especially after a perilous one. The rafters of our cottage gleamed warmly in the firelight that night, and Mousse lay at his ease in the warmth of the timber fire on our wide, welcoming hearth.

CHAPTER XXIV

The Storm-Petrel in Jeopardy

There are certain limits to safe boating on the open sea, and the more often one touches those limits the more careful one becomes to avoid them. In other words, experience teaches us caution, and, in John's favourite dict, 'It's better to make sure than to be sorry.' I shall never again moor my boat off in the haven overnight, and in winter.

It happened that the morning was calm one winter's day, when we went across to the mainland, and when returning to the island again a northerly breeze sprang up to help us. We sailed home swiftly before the wind, arriving back barely three hours after having left in the morning, and with all our mainland business done for the week.

When the wind is in the north, the south facing South Haven of our island is as tranquil as the traditional millpond. The fiercest northerly gale cannot make rough the sheltered water below the high walls of the landing-place. Therefore we pray often for northerly breezes, but get them rarely in winter, at least no longer than for a casual day at a time.

So quiet and smooth was South Haven that day that I decided we would leave the boat at her moorings. At that time we had a cork buoy marking the mooring chain and anchor. An endless rope ran from a block on this chain to the ring-bolt on the cliff and back again, and the method was to bend the boat's painter on to this rope; the boat could then be run from the cliff to the buoy on the endless rope after landing, and vice versa when we wished to embark. But this type of mooring was exposed to the water all the time; the ropes soon rotted, and, as we found subsequently, the first big southerly gale swept everything completely away. The moorings, however, had stood during and since the summer until the day of which I speak.

Dusk soon comes down on November days, and on this occasion the wind died away until there was but a faint breeze from the north. John and I looked down from the landing at the moored *Storm-Petrel* lying listlessly on the calm water. Surely it was safe to leave her for one night thus, while the breeze was in the north? How many times had we left her moored in the summer. We remembered that in one year there had been a period of days so calm that the boat had never once been berthed on the island slip for a whole month. Perhaps we were in for another calm spell? We agreed there could be no harm in leaving her for this one night, so we saluted her in the dusk and bade her good-night. There she lay, with all her gear neatly stowed along the thwarts: her sails, her mast and her oars. We left her sleeping on the water, and we ourselves went to bed later, confident that all was well; tired with the day's work and ready to sleep.

It was five in the morning when I woke to hear the loud moan of a strong wind. For a moment I listened, trying to make out the direction of the wind, expecting that the northerly breeze had freshened. In that case, of course, all would still be well. But was it north? It seemed to be pressing and moaning on the slates on the south roof of the house. Moreover, the east-facing bedroom window was whistling as the wind pressed upon it. I knew then that it was the dreaded south-east wind that was freshening: the hostile wind that so quickly blows into South Haven and raises mountainous seas there.

John, Richard and Henry dwell in a rehabilitated cottage next to the Wheelhouse. I expected the watchful John would already have heard the wind and thought of the boat, and when I ran out to the cottage I found him stirring up his companions. In the darkness we all felt our way down to South Haven. At every moment the wind was increasing, and with it my anxiety.

I think my heart missed several beats when I first peered down into the white foam of the sea in South Haven and saw no dark shape of my boat dancing on the water. How much I valued and cared for the *Storm-Petrel* I realized then. It seemed to me that I was facing the greatest disaster in my life, for a swift fleeting memory of all the sunny voyages she had given us came to me.

In the darkness before the late dawn, however, my eyes had deceived me, for when we all got down near the landing-steps we could see the precious boat bravely afloat and straining at her moorings as she rode up and down over the foaming waves which the wind drove in past her. Great was my relief!

To get at her was a different matter. It was not yet high water, but the waves splashed so high on the cliff where the mooring rope was fastened that neither John nor I could get down to unfasten it. Even had we been able to do so, it would still have been impossible in the darkness to get down over the wave-beaten rocks and jump aboard. We were compelled to wait for daylight.

The wind, now steadily rising to gale force, roared up the ravine of the haven and was bitterly cold. We were therefore glad to drink the hot tea Doris brought us. It warmed us a little as we crouched against the cliff, our eyes watching, between the showers of salt spray, for the moorings to part and let the *Storm-Petrel* be smashed on the rocks below us.

Dawn and high-water came together. We could barely see the ropes now, for the heavy seas were constantly over them. But still the *Storm-Petrel* rode the smother, head-on to wind and breakers. Each time she slanted up the wave, and then headlong down it, my heart plunged with her. I expected her every moment to bury her nose into the slant of the next close-rising wave, but she never quite plunged under. The most anxious moments were those when she slewed round a little, edging broadside-on in the trough of the waves. How the sea shook her then. Furiously to and fro it tossed and rocked her, making her now wallow in the trough and now pitch lengthwise on the breaking top. When half-broadside on she shipped water heavily, and it was with great relief that I saw her move to a head-on position again.

But this could not go on. More and more water was

splashing inboard until she was half-full. Her movements gradually grew heavy and sluggish; she did not ride so well, but plunged sullenly, taking every curl of foam and wave-crest inboard. We saw—I almost in despair—her stern sheets and loose wooden parts floating about inside her and the engine quite under water.

To swim out to her would be madness; the waves would overwhelm one if the first plunge did not end in striking the rocks. It seemed we must watch her sink at her moorings, and, certainly, any boat less seaworthy than the broad-beamed *Storm-Petrel* would have done so.

When at last there was perceptible evidence of the ebb, and we could see the rope more often John and I climbed down to the ring-bolt. As we unfastened the rope wave after wave dashed upon us, and as each one came we held desperately on to the cliff face.

John was the hero of this episode. Well-used to rock-climbing, at which pursuit he reminds me of a fly upon a perpendicular wall, he stood waiting for the chance to make a flying leap into the boat. I manoeuvred the ropes, gradually pulling the boat, and as near as I dared, into the cliff. Then, when there seemed to be at last a small interval between the pounding waves I yelled 'Ready!' and pulled the boat in hard. John, standing twenty feet above the water, ran headlong down over the sharp, steep cliff and made a brave and spectacular leap into the boat. Instantly I pulled on the reverse rope and gradually worked the boat out into the middle of the haven, away from the treacherous rocks.

John's weight, plus the water she had taken aboard, nearly sank the *Storm-Petrel.* As it was I had to warn him not to stand anywhere except amidships. I could see the water pouring in through the engine exhaust outlets, as the gunwale came level with the water, and that the oars and gear were about to float away. I shouted warnings, but am doubtful if he heard them in the noise of wind and wave, also he was expending all his energies upon bailing.

The small bailing scoop seemed ridiculously inadequate to remove hundreds of gallons of water, and for many minutes it seemed that he could not gain upon the amount of water still being dashed in. Up and down he was tossed with the boat as she rode heavily on the waves. I could feel the heavy strain of her weight on the mooring rope when I touched it with my hands. At any moment it must go. It was badly chafed in several places by the rocks already, and just as John had gained on the water in the boat with his scoop the mooring-rope chafed right through.

John was now satisfied that he could bail her out, and began to scoop out with less frenzied movements. When he saw that the rope had parted he tied the broken ends to the boat in order to stop them running out of the block on the mooring chain and continued to finish his job. Then he cast off the ropes, swung a paddle in the stern and sculled into the comparative shelter of the slipway. Even here, however, there were breaking waves, and it needed both of us to hold the *Storm-Petrel* on the slip until the cable on the winch, operated by Richard and Henry, at last dragged the boat to safety.

Never again have I moored the boat overnight in winter.

CHAPTER XXV

A November Gale

November and December are the months of the greatest storms and rains here. January is quieter; February generally cold with dry, easterly winds. Thereafter, March, April and May are often the quietest months of the year. During three winters the worst gales we have experienced have come in November.

It was in mid-November of the second winter that a terrific hurricane struck the island. For a whole week there had been south-westerly gales, until, on the fifteenth of the month, they abated and left only light airs from the west.

In spite of this lightness of wind, however, there was a very heavy ground-sea rolling in from the Atlantic, and, by dashing upon the cliffs of Mad Bay, and about the lighthouse, sent as much spray over the island as if a gale were actually blowing.

The crossing John and I made that day was not entirely to my liking. I felt a bit doubtful of the immense ground-seas which rolled majestically through the Broad Sound. Here and there, in spite of the lack of wind, where a rock or shoal rose within a dozen fathoms of the surface, the wave-crests would break in long, white array. A boat would stand no chance if such a crest broke upon it, and, therefore, we kept well away from any shallow ground.

When we passed through Jack Sound we chose a middle course; we dare not pass near the cliffs where the wash of the sea was terrific. Even the usually quiet waters of Martinshaven were agitated, and we had to choose the right moment between breaking waves at which to run aground.

A good illustration of a ground-sea may be had by breathing or blowing hard upon the surface of a bath of water. The disturbed surface is at once marked by widening circles of ripples, which travel far and wide over a big area before gradually diminishing in height and dying away until they are imperceptible. These ripples, which correspond to the swell of a ground-sea caused by a blow of wind, dash against the sides of the bath just as the swell does against the cliffs. It indicates that somewhere the water has been disturbed by wind, and that a gale is, or has been, in the vicinity. When these swells gradually lessen in height and strength you may feel easier in mind that the storm has passed away from your neighbourhood.

Now on this occasion they continued so to increase, to roar louder and wilder on the coasts, that John and I hurried to return to the island before the approaching gale arrived. I was very glad when we at last got into South Haven, using the motor only; for there was less wind than ever in the afternoon. With so little wind it would have been impossible to sail, for the swells so rocked the boat that the sails would have done nothing but shake and flap. From the crest of one swell to the crest of the next is a distance of perhaps fifty yards, while the height, reckoned from the bottom of the troughs to the crests, is about fifteen feet; though it seems nearer thirty when one sinks down into the trough and can see nothing but the slopes of the swells on each side. These measurements of an Atlantic swell, when running before a gale, are of course only an approximate calculation.

The swells always come in from the ocean out westward. They strike on the extreme westerly points of Mad Bay and the Head, and roll along the north and south cliffs until they re-unite eastward of the island. Because of this South Haven escapes the direct pounding of these swells, sheltered as it is by rocks and cliffs from the west. Excepting, therefore, when the south-east wind blows into the harbour we can always launch the boat, for the roll of the swells is a little checked by the sheltering cliffs, and is therefore much less by the time it reaches the boat-slip. Nevertheless, there are some days even when this roll is too high and rough to allow the boat to be handled, and when we got back that afternoon we had a very ticklish few minutes in hauling the *Storm-Petrel* up the slip. It had been bad enough launching with a full cargo in the morning, but now, when we ran upon the slip, the sea left us dry at one moment and at the next floating atop of the seas that rushed in. I am sure no lifeboat crew could better us now in handling, launching, and landing a boat in heavy seas upon our own slip.

All that night we could hear the great thunder as of a thousand distant guns booming. It was the ground-sea crashing on the cliffs, and the sound was very clear on the windless night air.

In the morning a gale from south-east was raging: a good solid ordinary sou'easter with hurrying dark clouds. Then the sky suddenly cleared and the wind veered to south-west. But it began to blow in earnest just before noon, and reached its greatest force at noon. I have never felt, or seen, anything so furious and wild as that hurricane.

The shriek of the wind gradually rose to a high whistle, which shrilled in my ears to the exclusion of all other sounds. Although I was standing within a few feet of a two-foot thick wall, and which was blown down in front of my eyes, I heard not a sound of the crashing masonry. Some twelve-feet of this wall, nine feet high, was blown out of one of the farm-folds, and almost immediately afterwards a similar-sized section was blown out of a fold-wall next to the Wheelhouse, carrying with it the corner stones of the Wheelhouse itself.

There are times when we think of the sea and the wind as sweet, clean and kind things; merciful to man and his possessions. But that is when there are calm days, or light summer breezes, and perhaps when the sea is warm and teeming with fish life. Yet, though we may love wind and sea, we learn to know that they have no pity for us; that they never think of us, and that they are hard and cruel; as ready to destroy utterly, as to bestow generously, when we encounter them. To-day sea and wind came tearing and shrieking at the island with intent to kill and destroy.

By no means satisfied with toppling over two high

walls, the gale sought to lift off every roof. It screamed in the slates of the house until I grew anxious; but when building I had riveted the edge of every slate to its neighbour and not a slate moved on the main roof. But in spite of its solid walls, in places three feet thick, the house quivered with the strength of the gale, and the roar all about the outside walls was terrific.

The roofs of the Wheelhouse and of the house-porch are tiled with island stone, and soon there were many gaps, for the heavy tiles came flying off at several points. The corrugated-iron roof of the cottage and store-rooms we just managed to save by piling immense stones, as much as three of us could lift together, upon it.

The house and all the buildings enjoy some shelter from the south-west by the configuration of the land in that direction. We wondered what it must be like at the lighthouse, which stood shelterless directly in the path of the gale. Later we learned that the sea had been battering to the top of the cliff, 100 feet high, running into the yards and down the mouth of the foghorn at the top of the building. The heavy wooden fence round the gardens, which lie sheltered behind an outcrop of rock, was destroyed, and the vegetables withered up. So, too, were our own green things, and covered with a thick crust of salt, even in our sheltered gardens. And beyond this the long grass of the bog was torn up bodily and blown in drifts into the yards and folds, while most of it was carried away entirely, rising higher and higher into the blue sky.

While this gale was at its height the sky was clear, excepting for an occasional, racing, white wisp of cloud, but as night came on, and the wind abated considerably, heavy clouds came up. We hauled the boat up to the very wheel of the winch. South Haven was a sad sight, presenting to us a mass of jagged, ugly rocks instead of a smooth beach of pebbles for landing on. The sea had washed all the pebbles out below low water, and we knew it would be months before they would be gradually washed back again.

For more than a week afterwards the sea continued to leap twenty feet above the topmost point of the Stack, and there was no venturing out upon it.

CHAPTER XXVI

Hard Times for the Birds

So far February has each year been a month when easterly winds have prevailed; the coldest month of the year. We do not mind these cold winds, which blow from off the land, as they bring us calm seas and dry weather after the winter storms. Not often does it rain from the east, and rarely are there flurries of snow. The only snow we have had in three winters came in February, 1928—our second winter—but it came then all at once and in earnest.

In the middle of the month frosts set in. As a rule frost rarely visits the island with any severity but now, for four days, there were intense frosts, which held the ground very hard. At the same time there were extremely bitter winds from east and south-east. So rough were these that they caused rough water even on the ponds, and thus prevented them from freezing over.

With the intense cold came great flocks of westward-flying birds. An east wind always brings us more visitors in the winter, and now, day after day, hundreds of starlings, thrushes, redwings, fieldfares, lapwing and golden plover arrived; snipe and jack snipe, too; woodcock, curlew, blackbirds, meadow-pipits, larks, wrens, robins, linnets, chaffinches and greenfinches in small flocks. On the edges of the two ponds widgeon, mallard and teal congregated, and once or twice small skeins of geese joined them.

Many of these visitors did not stop long, but hurried on westwards into the limitless Atlantic, some heading in a direction that would eventually land them in America, if they did and could continue so far; others made towards Grassholm, and in a northerly direction towards Ireland. The larks, pipits and starlings usually flew very low over the waves; the lapwing, curlew and golden plover flying very high in the air, often so high as barely to be seen and recognized.

Indeed, on a previous occasion—December 17th, 1927—I saw immense flocks of lapwing crossing at considerable height in a due west direction, flying at tremendous speed before a south-easterly gale. A few days later many lapwing were noticed on the east coast of Canada, where they perished in the cold and snow; and I often think that these may have been some of the very birds that flew over the island so precipitately before the bitter gale, and failing to touch Ireland at all may have continued onwards on a two-thousand mile flight to Newfoundland, where most of these birds were first seen.

The frozen state of the ground made it a difficult matter for the great numbers of birds to find food, and the strong penetrating winds added to their misery. Starlings dug at the hard ground unavailingly, and had to turn their attention to investigating the frosted tufts of grass. Snipe squatted by the frozen edges of the streams without having any 'visible means of sustenance.' The small finches alone were able to live comfortably on the seeds of grass and weeds. We fed as much as we could spare of corn and bread to the birds, but it was impossible to feed anything but the merest fraction of such an army. For the lapwing and golden plover, which seemed to suffer most, we could do nothing; they would not eat corn or bread.

On the fifteenth of the month, and after four days of intense frost, a heavy fall of snow covered the island more than a foot deep during the dark hours of the morning. It was fine, dry, powdery snow, and was blown by the wind into drifts four or five feet deep. The high, open places were almost swept clean by the wind and the exposed rises of the meadows were likewise swept. Here the birds sought for food in the face of the bitter wind, and, I think, obtained almost nothing.

Probably a number of birds arrived on the island already in poor condition at this time, for at inland places on the mainland the snow had been much more heavy and the cold more intense. At any rate this fall of snow on the island brought to our very door scores of weak and dying birds. It was saddening to find, on the day after the snowstorm, birds crowding for shelter into the farm fold and buildings, many barely able to fly more than a few yards.

Another day passed during which much of the snow had been blown away, but it was still freezing. The birds were now hand tame through hunger and cold. Lapwings, unable to fly and barely able to utter a feeble call, tottered unsteadily behind the high walls of the folds. Golden plover were in worse case, many dying at our door, whilst others crouched down on the very step. We carried some indoors, but the warmth of the room seemed to have an adverse effect on them, hurrying their death by a few hours. Each bird we carried in seemed to droop instantly—the transition from intense cold to the neighbourhood of a fire in a room proved too much for them. They breathed very quickly for a few moments, drooped their heads and died, one and all; lark, robin, starling, hedge-sparrow and plover. We could do no more, though the birds seemed to be seeking our help in the way they crowded about the house, the buildings and the home-meadows.

It was at this time that we had several tame rabbits living in outdoor pens, and the does were already busy rearing their nestsfull of young in the shelters provided for them. By day the hungry birds stole and fought over the rabbits' corn and roots, and at night they crept into the inner compartments of the hutches, nestling down among the baby rabbits and against the bodies of the does for the sake of the warmth. It was a strange sight to open a hutch and find the doe brooding a family consisting of her own furry offspring and a batch of perhaps six to a dozen starlings, thrushes or blackbirds. Sometimes a wren or a hedge-sparrow would be there. In the mornings the birds would straggle out to face the world once more and seek food, but often they left their weaker comrades behind. Each day I had to remove a certain number of birds which had succumbed in the hutches overnight.

Farther afield, away from the buildings, the crows and gulls, at least, were not starving. They had plenty of victims for the trouble of knocking them over, though it is true that such fare was a scant one of feathers and bones, so miserably emaciated were their victims.

On the sea, when on a calm day we crossed to the mainland, we saw several flocks of larks and starlings flying very weakly and low over the water. Many must have fallen into the sea on their voyages, unable to continue the exertion of beating their wings. Martinshaven beach was lined with dead birds. We saw one song-thrush hovering over the water as if it thought to alight on an imaginary stone; there was no stone there, however, and the exhausted bird sank into the sea, to be drowned at once.

Even some of the robbers perished. We found several dead and dying herring gulls and two great black-backs, as well as many dead crows. We lost our beloved pair of stonechats, and it was not for a whole year that we regained a pair in their place on the island. There was one lady chaffinch who had but one eye; she lived comfortably at night in the corn-bin, flying in when I opened the door, and in the morning she shared the chickens' food with Jonathan and Co., many starlings and small birds.

The weather broke early in March, at least enough to thaw the ground, and the sun shone often. The birds recovered strength with amazing celerity, and in a few days the feeble calls and tottering flight of the golden plover were changed to their normal sharp whistle and swift direct flight. The shearwaters, banished by the cold after an early arrival in February, returned in great strength. The oyster-catchers rattled off their spring alarums, selecting the sites for their nests, each pair strictly to a well-defined territory of its own, on the high outcrops of rock in all the meadows.

Not many days later came the wheatears and an early chiffchaff, as well as that rarer visitor, the black redstart. Once more the dread winter was over and sweet spring here again.

CHAPTER XXVII

Happily Ever After

Certainly early spring and summer is the sweetest time of the island year, when each day brings more sunshine, birds and flowers. Life then is one long round of busy pleasure.

The first lambs of the flock of sheep I now have come in February, and the majority have arrived by the end of March. Shepherding is full of interest and expectation at this time. I walk each day around the island, counting the flock and tending the ewes with lambs; making sure that they have sought shelter on windy days, and that all is well. I confess it is an easy task, and much to my liking, this long perambulation along the cliffs, counting my precious flock, and welcoming the new-born lambs and seeing that they are able to stand sturdily on their long legs and take nourishment.

The sheep are quite wise to the weather, and save me much trouble by always retiring to the lee side of the island in bad weather. Here, behind rock outcrops, and on the cliff slopes they have perfect shelter from the wind. They graze happily on the coarse grass, campion and thrift. Because we keep no hurrying, worrying dogs the sheep are very tame, as are our goats; and we have little trouble in examining them at any time. The flock, which increases each year, numbers about fifty, headed by his majesty Crag, the black-faced ram. They are mostly of the hardy Welsh mountain breed, well suited to grazing on rough, exposed land.

In walking every day around the island upon this work I am able to satisfy my desire to know how my little kingdom progresses, what new arrivals are here, what birds gone: whether the tadpoles are hatched under the starwort in the main pond, whether the lesser black-backs have yet occupied the bog, whether the ravens have brought their young off, whether any more black redstarts have come, whether the vernal squills, the campion or the cowslips are flowering, and a hundred other events of early spring. In summer the thousand daily events and adventures of the walk are almost bewildering. On hot days, when the long walk over rough ground and through bracken and heather—perhaps for four miles—following the indentations of the coastline, is likely to exhaust too much energy and time, the pony is saddled, and the rounding-up is accomplished at a gallop.

Time is precious in summer. Early in the morning John and I drive in the flock to the folds before breakfast, and while the grass is yet wet with dew. First one of us gallops off to the end of the island on Punch, and drives in the outlying ewes and half-grown lambs, while the other, on foot, brings in the nearer sheep. Punch is of a mountain breed, like the sheep, and knows how to gallop over rough ground and how to recover his balance, if he steps into a rabbit-hole, without throwing his rider. Once in the main fold the flock is examined with the eye for signs of fly-attacks, counted, and then released. In June comes shearing-time, and from July onwards the unwanted lambs and ewes are sold off to dealers on the mainland.

When we have examined the sheep, and have had breakfast, the main work of the day begins. We hurry off to the day's fishing, eager to see what wondrous things of the sea we have caught in our basket pots, and all day long we are in the boat at this pleasant task. Though the hauling up of the pots is not light work, it is extremely fascinating to peer into each pot to see what Neptune has given us. The pots are each baited with three pieces of gurnet for the snaring of lobsters, crayfish and crabs, and, although we get our fair share of these, we also have many unexpected hauls of such fish as conger-eels, cuttle-fish, jelly-fish, star-fish, sea-slugs, prawns, 'spider' and other strange crabs, and many another strange-looking denizen of the deep.

The pots, which we ourselves make out of withies, in the slack period at the end of winter, are tied on a long line, twelve to each 'string'. The ends of the string are then buoyed with corks, to mark the spot where the string is 'shot' into the water. The pots themselves are each weighted with two stones to make them sink to the bed of the sea. We work six of these strings, a total of seventy-two pots, shot at various points around the island-coast, hauling all of them as often as four times each day in favourable weather. Sometimes Doris accompanies John and me, especially when we try our luck farther afield and shoot a string of pots at Grassholm. Once a week the accumulated catch of shell-fish is taken to the mainland and marketed.

From our goats we obtain milk, butter and cheese; from our garden, fruit and the produce of the soil; from the chickens and gulls, eggs; from the island and the sea, rabbits and fish. We have only to grow and grind our own wheat in order to be self-supporting. I have even suggested to Doris that we spin our own wool and weave our own garments! So far, however, we rely on others, and I think for these we shall always do so, not being so entirely self-reliant that we desire to discard the advantages and conveniences of civilization.

From the sea we obtain our firewood. So far the coal from the schooner has lasted us three years, and I think will hold out for another five. If we do not have another wreck by the end of that time we shall dig peat from the 'turbary' on the bog. This 'turbary', an area of a few acres, supplied the fuel of turf or peat which the inhabitants of the island used over a hundred years ago.

The talk of peat brings me thus late to the history of the island, of which very little appears to be known. Fenton, in his *Tour Through Pembrokeshire*, of 1811, describes the house as having been built in a 'whimsical manner, with suitable farm offices' by a gentleman. He offers no date of building, but from what little evidence I can gather it must have been constructed not later than 1750, and probably earlier by some decades. The inhabitants of the farm in those days, when they stood in need of anything, lit a fire on a high rock as a signal for a boat to attend them. If they required flour for bread they lit the fire on a high rock in the centre of the island; this rock being known even now as Bread Rock; if urgent medical assistance was needed the fire was lit on the top of Spy Rock, the easternmost prominence as viewed from the mainland.

Those were days when telegraphy was almost unknown. Now, if we should ever be in dire need of medical aid, or other assistance, and it were impossible to use our boat at the time, we should have recourse to signalling the coastguards at St Ann's Head by means of a morse lantern, and could, if necessary, send a telegram at any time by such means.

Happily illnesses are unknown in this healthy, salt air. The coast-dwelling folk of Pembrokeshire have a reputation for longevity, and I like to picture myself an old salt, with a flowing white beard, and at eighty years of age still hauling my pots and driving my sheep. But Doris, as yet, does not approve of a beard.

Thus you will see my one-time dreams have come true, for I dwell on an island, far from the turmoil of a city, and accessible only to the chosen few. I have all the birds I could wish for, and welcome every one. In the summer I can reckon there are over thirty thousand on our island, of which two-thirds comprise puffins and shearwaters. In variety, so far, over a hundred different species are recorded, and there is a peculiar delight in welcoming new species; more particularly in such a well-defined area as an island.

Each summer brings us fresh cruising adventures, and when the North wind is true and steady we shall be sailing once more out to far distant Grassholm to see again the gannets and seals.

And so live happily ever after!

Index

Admiral, 13, 20, 71
Alice, 52, 64, 106
Alice Williams, 52, 55, 61, 65, 137
America, 14, 154
Atlantic, 13, 60, 83, 116, 138, 147, 154
Azores, 12

Bear Island, 11
Billy, 61
Bishops, the, 96
Bishop, the Little, 99
 the Middle, 97
 the North, 97
 the South, 99
Boar's Bay, 43
Bread Rock, 163
Bristol Channel, the, 12
Broad Sound, the, 16, 83, 104, 147

Canada, 154
Cleddau, the, 84
Clerks, the, 96
Columbus, 88
Crab Bay, 43
Crag, 160
Cristal, 60, 137
Crusoe, 11, 26

Dale, 87
Dale Roads, 136
Doris, 25, 67, 81 etc.
Dream Island, 25

Edward, 104
England, 86, 95

Faroes, 11, 73
Fenton, *Tour through Pembrokeshire*, 79, 162
Foxtrot, the, 16, 26, 32, 55 etc

Garland Stone, 85
Grassholm, 84, 87, 90, 97, 154, 162, 164
Great Castle Head, 137
Green Islet, the, 87

Haze, the, 35, 48
Head, the, 149
Hebrides, the, 11
Henry, 47, 55, 61 etc.
High Adventure, 47
High Seas, the, 47
Hy Brasail, 86

Iceland, 11, 73
Infant, the, 85, 127, 129, 134
Ireland, 86, 154

Jack Sound, 14, 16, 35, 38, 41, 48, 56, 83, 104, 108, 130, 148
Jan Mayen, 11

John, 16, 23, 31 etc
Jonathan, 67, 80, 157

Katherine, 67

Linney Head, 105
Little Sound, the, 56, 129, 134
Lockley, 31, 100
London Town, 53
Lower Island, the, 31, 50, 86, 132
  Lodge, 47
Lundy Island, 86

Macquarie, 12
Mad Bay, 24, 66, 149
Marloes, 15, 26, 30, 48, 55, 61, 76, 87, 110
Martinshaven, 16, 23, 35, 55, 59, 85, 103, 148, 157
Mason, the, 63
Matilda, 67
Mewstone Rock, 108
Midland Island, 56
Milford Dock, 136
  Haven, 38, 55, 84, 135
Molesey, SS, 109
Mountain, the, 80
Mousse, 137
Mull Island, 11

Neptune, 161
Newfoundland, 154
North Ronay, 11

Orkneys, the, 11

Pembrokeshire, 13, 31
Peter's Bay, 43
Promised Lands, 84
Punch, 160

Ramsey Island, 12, 94
  Sound, 96, 101
Relief, the, 101
Rhode Islanders, 67
Richard, 34, 36, 44 etc
Royal Society for the Protection of Birds, the, 102
Rufus, 67
Rye Rocks, 129

St Ann's Head, 41, 55, 60, 109, 135, 163
  Lighthouse, 38
St Bride's Bay, 82, 115, 127
  Castle, 82
  Haven, 82
St David's, 109
St George's Channel, 114, 136
St Martin's, 132
Sandy Haven, 60, 136
Savages, the, 12
Scotland, 86
Shetlands, the, 11
Skokholm, 14, 25, 30, 38, 50
Skomer, 12, 16, 31, 38, 56, 85, 92, 95, 108, 127
  North Haven, 59, 128
Skye, 11
Sounds, the, 32, 96, 127
South Haven, 23, 28, 32, 41, 43, 49, 66, 104, 148
Spitzbergen, 11
Spy Rock, 50, 81, 163
Stack, the, 39, 106, 129, 152
Steepholm, 12
Storm-Petrel, the, 34, 39, 43, 55, etc

Thoreau, 12, 20, 47
Tidball Rock, 106
Tristan d'Acunha, 12
Tuskar Rock, 135

Upper Island, 31

Wales, 13, 86, 95
Wheelhouse, the, 70, 142, 150
Wooltack Point, 35, 109